PREACHING

FROM THE

OLD

TESTAMENT

WALTER BRUEGGEMANN

Fortress Press

Minneapolis

For Ellen Davis

TABLE OF CONTENTS

FOREWORD

There has been no greater Old Testament theologian in the last half century than Walter Brueggemann. A few have his equal, but none has eclipsed his contributions to the field. No Old Testament theologian has produced scholarship exceeding either the quality or the quantity that has flowed from his pen (literally, from his pen). Walter has so enriched and inspired the preaching of the church.

At Working Preacher, we believe that biblical preaching changes lives. This is true for many reasons, but primarily, biblical preaching changes lives because God meets and changes people when the Bible is preached as a living word, through which the living God acts. Walter shares those commitments. His servant scholarship has helped multitudes of preachers engage with the Old Testament in ways that have encouraged faithful and fresh proclamation of the ancient word in the modern and now postmodern world. For all of those reasons, it is an honor to have Walter Brueggemann as the author of the inaugural volume in the new series Working Preacher Books. Thank you, Walter.

Forty years ago, in what may be Walter Brueggemann's most significant book, *The Prophetic Imagination* (Fortress Press, 1978), he opened with an incredible rhetorical salvo: "The contemporary American church is so largely enculturated to the American ethos of consumerism that it has little power to believe or to act" (p. 11). Stop for a moment and reflect on that breathtaking diagnosis. Because the church was syncretized to *American consumerism, it had little power to believe or act!*

He continued, "Our consciousness has been claimed by false fields of perception and idolatrous systems of language and rhetoric." That enculturation had resulted in a "loss of identify through the abandonment of the faith tradition . . . [resulting in] a depreciation of memory and a ridicule of hope" (p. 11).

In response to that diagnosis, Brueggemann prescribed an "urgent" recovery of the faith tradition via a "prophetic ministry." This prophetic ministry was to avoid the fundamentalisms of both the right and the left—or, better, to gather the wisdom and insights of both the right and the left—like those scribes of the kingdom who bring out what is both old and new from the treasure house. "The task of prophetic ministry," he asserted, "is to nurture, nourish, and evoke a consciousness and perception alternative to the consciousness and perception of the dominant culture around us" (p. 13). This "alternative" consciousness was to address the crisis "of having our alternative vocation co-opted and domesticated" while at the same time living "in fervent anticipation of the newness that God has promised and will surely give."

The prophetic ministry that Brueggemann prescribed can be understood as a ministry of rhetoric—a particular type of preaching and witnessing that speak a "prophetic imagination" into existence. This rhetoric takes many different forms:

* Israel's "groans and laments" that began to dismantle oppressive structures.
* The "doxologies of the new community" that imagined a different consciousness.

✳ Jeremiah's conjured "funeral and bringing the grief of dying Israel to public expression."

✳ Second Isaiah practiced *"radical energizing* [of hope] against the royal consciousness."

✳ Jesus "practiced criticism of the deathly world around him" through his parables, controversies, and in his crucifixion and resurrection.

To this we could add the lamentation of Amos, the marriage and children's names of Hosea and Gomer, the wedding song of Isaiah of Jerusalem, the courtroom indictment of Micah, the song of hope of Habakkuk, the wisdom of Proverbs and Qohelet, the prayer and praises of the psalm, and more. This prophetic rhetoric in all of its diversity and creativity was "to evoke an alternative community" of the evangelical imagination (see pp. 109–11).

Fast-forward forty years—a biblical number. Now crack the cover of Brueggemann's latest book—a book on preaching from the Old Testament—and we find our venerable, trusted teacher essentially equipping and encouraging us in the same defiant and hopeful rhetoric of evangelical imagination. He has stayed up-to-date on current hermeneutical and historiographical conversations (such as empire studies and the like). He has continued to track the ideology of the marketplace, which exerts an even more seductive influence than it did forty years ago. This new volume is not repacking or merely updating his older work—it is more of a capstone, crowning his long career of serving preachers as they seek to preach from the Old Testament.

In this new volume, Brueggemann explores and equips the reader to preach from Genesis (chapter 1), from the long tale of Moses (chapter 2), from the prophets (chapter 3), from the psalms (chapter 4), and from the Old Testament wisdom traditions (chapter 5). In these chapters, Brueggemann acknowledges that each of the different genres and theologies of the Old Testament requires different homiletical approaches. He expertly leads his readers into the theologies, genres, and histories of the various genres, while also equipping them to emerge from those ancient texts ready to engage in what he calls the "hard, glorious work of preaching."

Walter—For this new project and for all you have done to teach and inspire, we give thanks. On behalf of all your readers and students, please accept our heartfelt gratitude.

Thank you.

And thank God for you.

Rolf A. Jacobson
Advent 2018

PREFACE

The Old Testament is perennially, at the same time, a rich resource and a complex challenge for the Christian preacher. In this book I have refused grand theological schemes in response to that complex challenge and have focused instead on what is in front of us in the text. This means I have not been drawn to a "law gospel" articulation or to a "promise fulfillment" scheme, the two structures that have most often occupied interpreters. I believe, moreover, that a Christian sermon based on an Old Testament text does not need finally to make a direct Christological connection. I make that judgment on two counts. First, the Christian liturgy in which the sermon is embedded assures a context for the sermon of Trinitarian affirmation. Second, the God attested in the Old Testament is indeed the God of the gospel so that it is sufficient to let the good news take the form of witness to the God of the text.

I seek to show Christian preachers that the faith witnessed in these several traditions provide connections to our contemporary faith challenges that are myriad, rich, and suggestive. I also assume that a wholesale sustained engagement with the Old Testament is worth the effort for the preacher. I recognize the sorry fate of Old Testament texts in the Revised Common Lectionary that constitutes a major disservice for the church and its preachers. The lectionary variously bowdlerizes and gerrymanders the

Old Testament to make it serve other claims, most of the time not allowing it to have its own evangelical say. It is my hope that my exposition here might evoke and energize fresh homiletical attention to the Old Testament, precisely because I believe the urgent work of the gospel in our society requires attentive listening to these ancient voices of bold insistent faith.

Broadly I have been led by genre analysis, that is, a recognition that the several elements of the Old Testament canon are cast in a variety of genres. While form criticism has most often focused on smaller units of the text, we can without doubt see that the larger units of the canon are cast in a variety of genres, and each genre—narrative, commandment, poem, saying, and so on—can carry only the freight that is appropriate to it. So, my intent is to elucidate some of the resources that are available to the preacher when attention is paid to the work of the text itself, without imposing extrinsic theological categories or expectations on the text.

I am glad to acknowledge the cruciality of preaching for the life, faithfulness, and well-being of the church. I take it that every sermon has as its elemental purpose the formation, maintenance, nurture, and empowerment of a Christian congregation engaged in baptismal mission. Such preaching is exceedingly difficult and challenging, because any faithful preaching of baptismal mission is deeply countercultural in a society like ours that is accustomed to instrumental reasoning, individual autonomy, and commodification that disregards the common good. Because of its countercultural impulse, preaching is both profoundly urgent and deeply problematic among us. This book is offered as support for and as a salute to my many faithful fellow preachers, some of whom are my mentors, some of whom are my students, all of whom are my companions.

I am glad to dedicate this book to Ellen Davis, my long-time companion in Old Testament study. Since her publication of *Imagination Shaped: Old Testament Preaching in the Anglican Tradition* (1995), I have known that Ellen lives between the guild and the church, with her critical work fully in the service of the community of faith. That, of course, is the space I always intend to occupy. I am glad we share that passion. Ellen, moreover, has been a generous supportive colleague to me over time, and I am grateful.

I am glad to thank Scott Tunseth and his colleagues at Fortress Press for their willingness to take up this manuscript. Fortress Press has for the longest time been my go-to press, and I am glad for this publication at the end of my work. I am grateful for colleagues at the press, in the church, and in the academy who have permitted me the freedom and given me support for the work of exposition represented here.

Walter Brueggemann
October 20, 2018

1

Preaching from the Torah: Genesis

The book of Genesis is something of an outlier in the Torah. It does not easily connect to the Moses narrative that is to follow. It is always and everywhere "beforehand." It is before the confrontation with Pharaoh and the departure from Egypt. It is before the crisis and wonders of the wilderness. It is before the meeting at Sinai and the requirements of covenant. It is before the elongated preaching that Moses offers at the Jordan boundary.

It is, in sum, beforehand, because it seeks to make a beginning. We may imagine the makers of this text pondering the most effective ways to begin this narrative that will be a mix of fidelity and infidelity. These makers of text were variously collectors, borrowers, editors, and interpreters:

* They collected all sorts of material that may have been in oral form, mostly about family dealings.
* They were borrowers; quite clearly they were informed by and appropriated grand liturgical materials that were

commonly known and used in Near Eastern culture and liturgy.

* They were editors who selected (or excluded) materials and arranged them in this way rather than in some other way that was also possible.

* By the processes of collection, appropriation, and editing they gave theological interpretation to the quite diverse materials with which they worked, so that they were shaped into a more-or-less coherent, sustained narrative of beginnings.

Here Begins . . .

The book is entitled Genesis, that is, "beginnings," and in Hebrew it is *bereshith,* "in the beginning," the first word in the first verse. So we may ask, what is the beginning to which they testify? What began? Well, God did not begin here. But everything else began here, everything else evoked, generated, imagined, made by God's will and God's word and God's command and God's authority. Already everything other than God is set in a relationship to God without whom nothing was made that has been made.

Here begins the offer of a well-ordered shalom bearing the blessing of God and under mandate to generativity that assures the food chain and the human population. This is indeed "original blessing" wrought by God.[1]

Here begins the alienated practice of violence that will permeate all that follows. That practice of violence is rooted in the misdirected desire chronicled already in the garden of shalom. That practice of violence will surface against the brother (Genesis 4), against the environment (Genesis 6), and against the right ordering of the nations (Gen 11:1–9).

Here begins the anguished fidelity of God who must, in episode after episode, respond to alienating violence with a will to transpose self-inflicted curse into life-giving blessing.

Here begins chosenness. That beginning with Sarah and Abraham is as abrupt as the initial beginning of heaven and earth. God said, "Let there be light" (1:3). Later on, God said, "Go from your country" (12:1). The beginning as staged by the text comes as the edict of a potentate who expects to have the royal will immediately enacted. And then it is an imperative addressed to one person, Abraham. The text is arranged so that the torrent of cosmic beginnings is quickly focused on this particular familial beginning.

Here begins obedience to covenant that is foreshadowed in the righteousness of Noah: "So Abraham went." And this people is forever marked by the mandate to obey and so must live with the crisis of not fully obeying.

Here begins a preoccupation with the land, "The land that I will show you." And since all wars are elementally turf battles, here begins a dispute about the land. Very soon there was "strife" between those who herded livestock for Abraham and for Lot, and that ancient dispute has only grown more unbearably acrimonious in times since (13:7).

Here begin "wonders" that refuse to fit our narratives of explanation. The story turns finally on the birth of an heir; it pivots each time on the reality of barrenness. But then, belatedly, another birth is granted and the promise persists yet again.

Here begins the promise to the chosen; but what in fact begins is the endless problem of being chosen.[2] Why Abel and not Cain? Why Jacob and not Esau? Why with hands crossed, Ephraim and only then Manasseh?

Here begins hope (for land) that is endlessly contested, for it is always hope for land that belongs to someone else. Sometimes it is a hope accepted in obedience, sometimes it is hope excessively managed in disobedience. Here begins fidelity from God that evokes fidelity in response, but for both parties it is fidelity that is profoundly uneasy and fragile.

In short, this narrative sets in motion a way of being in the world that is inescapably filled with risk and therefore contestation. Many other ways of being in the world could be imagined, ways not so dependent upon wonders, not so scarred by disobedience, and not so tilted by chosenness. This, however, is what the text-makers have given us, an act of imagination that must have arisen out of and in the midst of real life, and yet an act of imagination that impinged upon real life from elsewhere, imposing its categories and insisting that all of life would perforce be thematized in this way, a way of wonder and engagement, of fidelity and infidelity.

At the moment, there is a strong scholarly advocacy that these text-makers—collectors, borrowers, editors, interpreters—completed their work in the Persian period (approximately 550–330 BCE). They had been at work for a very long time, but that seems now to be the time of completion. This consensus is the basis of our thinking, even if it is a consensus that will no doubt change in time to come. It is good enough for now. The Persian domination of that part of the world lasted from the defeat of Babylonia until the emergence of Alexander the Great and the coming of Hellenistic culture, a long two centuries. While the Persian regime is presented in the Old Testament as relatively benign compared to that of Babylonia, it was nonetheless an empire that treated Judah as a colony, and hosted Jews who had been forcibly transported from their homeland.[3] The purpose of maintaining a colony is to raise taxes that will support and enhance the central power. Thus Ezra, the scribe who led the recovery of Torah and who benefitted greatly from Persian governmental benevolence, can still say in his extended prayer:

> Here we are, slaves to this day—slaves in the land that you gave to our ancestors to enjoy its fruit and its good gifts. Its rich yield goes to the kings whom you have set over us because of our sins; they have power also over our bodies and over our livestock at their pleasure, and we are in great distress. (Neh 9:36–37)

This is a bitter complaint addressed to God concerning the economic status of Jews in Jerusalem under Persia: "slaves in our own land"! As with all slavery, the point is economic. The produce of labor in the land went to support the Persian kings who have power over their bodies and over their livestock (means of production), a summation not unlike that made in the book of Genesis when Joseph confiscated land and bodies of peasants on behalf of Pharaoh's food monopoly (Gen 47:13–26). The prayer ends, "We are in great distress!," literally, we are in a tight place; we are being squeezed.

This prayer of Ezra that ends in complaint begins with great doxology to YHWH. It first acknowledges YHWH as creator:

> You are the Lord, you alone, you have made heaven, the heaven of heavens, and all their host, the earth and all that is on it, the seas and all that is them. To all of them you give life, and the host of heaven worships you. (9:6)

Then the prayer alludes to Abraham:

> You are the Lord, the God who chose Abram and brought him out of Ur of the Chaldeans and gave him the name of Abraham; and you found his heart faithful

5

before you, and made with him a covenant to give to his descendants the land of the Canaanite, the Hittite, the Amorite, the Perizzite, the Jebusite, and the Girgashite; and you have fulfilled your promise, for you are righteous. (vv. 7–8)

These two beginning points, creation and Abraham, give us the two great themes of the book of Genesis. Creation attests YHWH's great power, the one worshipped by the host of heaven. The Abraham reference attests YHWH's fidelity in covenant.

The beginning and the end of Ezra's prayer identify the *circumstance of distress* in which the prayer is uttered and a *doxological tradition* concerning God's power and fidelity. To this we add the fact that Ezra promulgated the Torah:

[Ezra] helped the people to understand the law, while the people remained in their places. So they read from the book from the laws of God, with interpretation. They gave the sense, so that the people understood the reading. (Neh 8:7–8)

It is remarkable that in their distress the Jews read and interpreted Torah, which we take here to be the sum of the Pentateuch, the "Five books of Moses." Thus we may see that the Torah is an alternative, an answer, and an antidote to Persian-propelled distress. These three motifs in Ezra—*Torah interpretation, doxologies of creation and Abraham*, and *economic distress*—may provide a way for the preacher to think about the book of Genesis with its twin themes of creation and ancestors in covenant. In the wake of this text, our own tradition concerns interpretation (preaching) and doxology (praise), and our circumstance is acutely one of economic distress.

Empires prefer to erode or erase local identities, because local identities are at best an inconvenience to empire. So let us entertain the thought that Ezra, faced with the empire that wanted to erode or to erase local Jewish identity, countered that imperial impulse by declaring that Torah would function as the normative expression of local Jewish, covenantal identity. It is an identity that is grounded in a conviction of YHWH as powerful creator who is to be worshipped as faithful covenant partner of Abraham and his family. Torah is a refusal to give in to imperial identity and to maintain a distinct alternative identity.

An Analogy: The Market Ideology in Our Culture

Preachers always work by analogy. So let me trace out a possible analogue. Let us focus on the domination of market ideology in our culture. It is an ideology of immense political-economic force sustained by a widely accepted moral facade that dominates and controls our imagination, that administers the media and determines what we see and what we know, and that largely controls the government so that our public discourse is almost completely contained within its horizon. That market ideology exercises such a totalizing voice among us that it is difficult to imagine facets of life not under that purview. That market ideology is impatient—not to say inhospitable—toward all of those who do not fully participate in its requirements. It is impatient with those who do not practice the schemes of credit (so check your credit rating!), and it is inhospitable toward those who are unproductive, who contribute nothing and so do not have the wherewithal to purchase and consume. Such nonparticipants become nonpersons in the working of this ideology, an account of reality that contains and allows both liberal and conservative options. It sweeps all before it. Anything that cannot be slotted in its framework is dismissed as irrelevant or unreal.

In the face of such dominant forces, the maintenance of a distinct community with a distinct identity and a distinct purpose is difficult to sustain. But here, the practice of baptism regularly performed with water and the utterance of the divine name is alien to market ideology. The Episcopal tradition most poignantly marks the sacramental act with the deep claim, "You are sealed as Christ's own forever." This is an extraordinary claim, that you are marked, named, and destined for a different kind of life, a life defined by gospel tradition and not by the brands of market ideology. The rite of baptism is odd enough, as the empire reduces life to technique that has no appreciation for sign, symbol, or sacrament, except as a marketing tool. But odd as the rite is, it is the maintenance of peculiar baptismal identity that is the hard work and the challenge of the baptismal community and the peculiar responsibility of the preacher.

Thus I suggest, for our thinking about Christian preaching, that just as the Torah, in its completed form in the Persian period, provided Jews with a distinct narrative identity in the face of Persian domination, so the preaching task from Genesis is the maintenance of baptismal identity in the face of the life authorized and limited by market ideology. The Torah that centers on the awesome power and the abiding fidelity of God provides standing ground outside the massive claims of empire. The Torah is a testimony to life outside the dominant hegemony of empire, and a tool for articulating and maintaining that "life outside."

So who may be outside the domination of empire?

1. Well, surely first of all Jews. The Torah and the book of Genesis are for Jews. They are children of Abraham who are invited into promises that the dominant ideology cannot make and cannot keep.[4]

2. But we Christians claim the witness of Genesis as our own. It functions as our testimony to "life outside," and as a tool for articulating and maintaining that life outside. The majestic cadences of Genesis 1 are clearly echoed in the majestic cadences of the Fourth Gospel where we make the claim that the Son is at work with the Father in the work of creation:

> In the beginning was the Word, and the Word was with God, and the Word was God. He was in the beginning with God. All things came into being through him, and without him not one thing came into being. What has come into being in him was life, and the life was the light of all people. (John 1:1–2)

And then the church in its creed echoes:
Through him all things were made.

The creation is a gift given by the Father who is "Maker," we say, the Son through whom all things were made, the great work of the Spirit, the giver of life. The world could never derive from or be accountable to Persia. The creation could never be recruited from the management techniques of market ideology, because all creatures, as Ezra affirms, worship the creator and none other, along with the host of heaven (Neh 9:6).

And, of course, Paul can readily claim that the promise to Abraham, "All the Gentiles will be blessed in you," as the "gospel beforehand," the promise embodied by Jesus of Nazareth that reaches beyond the primal claim of Jews (Gal 3:8). Paul makes the claim that the promise to Abraham, from its initial utterance, concerned a reach to Gentiles.

3. But beyond Jews and Christians, those "outside," to whom the book of Genesis pertains, include all those who yearn for a sacramental existence, all those ready for covenant, all those who resolve to live by covenantal fidelity. More specifically, the book of Genesis functions as buoyancy for those excluded from or left behind by market ideology, all the vulnerable, the "unproductive," those without hope in the world who are reduced to a valueless commodity.

Note well, this is not an argument against the market or its proper function in the private sphere. The key is the term "ideology" that makes the grand claim that the market provides a master narrative that is deep and weighty and thick enough to be an ultimate account of reality. It is possible, given location in the Genesis tradition, to participate in the market without subscribing to its ideological pretensions, but in context it is exceedingly difficult to do so. The issue is joined frontally by Robert Jensen:

> We must summon the audacity to say that modernity's scientific/metaphysical metanarrative . . . is not the encompassing story within which all other accounts of reality must establish their place or be discredited by failing to find one. . . . As pop scientists urge over and over, the tale told by Scripture and creeds finds no comfortable place within modernity's metanarrative. It is time for the church to reply: This is certainly the case, and the reason it is the case is that the tale told by Scripture is too comprehensive to find place within so drastically curtailed a version of the facts. Indeed, the gospel story cannot fit within *any* other would-be metanarrative

because it is itself the only true metanarrative—or it is altogether false.[5]

It is the claim of market ideology to be a master narrative that is to be challenged. While I have focused on the domain of the market, Jensen focuses on Darwinism, but it is the same claim.

Against such pretense the book of Genesis—in the hands of Ezra—is a resistance against such ideology. More than that, it is an alternative. It is the hard, glorious work of preaching to bear witness, both as an act of resistance and as an act of alternative.

Self-Sufficiency and Sabbath

Every ambitious empire wants to imagine that it is ultimate and self-sufficient. So Pharaoh, according to Ezekiel, could boast:

> My Nile is my own;
> I made it for myself. (Ezek 29:3)

So Babylonia, according to Isaiah, could declare:

> I shall be mistress forever . . .
> I am, and there is no one besides me . . .
> No one sees me . . .
> I am, and there is no one besides me. (Isa 47:7, 8, 10)

We do not have such a boast from the lips of the Persians, but it is nonetheless fair to assume that they made the same claim. The boast of ultimacy (and therefore self-sufficiency) gives license to the empire to do whatever it pleases. For that reason we may imagine that every one of these empires (including the Persians) could stage great festivals of legitimacy that included a show of wealth and power that came liturgically with a warrant from God. Such a claim of ultimacy and self-sufficiency is, of course, inhospitable to any local identity. We may imagine that the Persian Empire, in its liturgic self-assertion, was inhospitable to Jewish identity, even as we can observe that the American empire, in its claim, is inhospitable to baptismal identity.

It is the work of the Torah to critique such a false claim of ultimacy and self-sufficiency, and to offer an alternative act of liturgic imagination that would sustain a distinct covenantal identity. One can see the critique concerning Babylonia in Second Isaiah. The exilic poet observes and mocks the ritual procession of the Babylonian gods:

> Bel bows down, Nebo stoops,
> Their idols are on beasts and cattle;
> these things you carry are loaded as burdens on weary
>   animals.
> They stoop, they bow down together;
> They cannot save their burden,
> but themselves go into captivity. (46:1–2)

These gods are portrayed as helpless, lifeless icons that must be carried along. The critique of the gods in Isaiah 46 is matched by the critique of imperial arrogance in chapter 47, already cited above.

And then the poet, providing grounding for Israel's covenantal identity in defiance against imperial hegemony, states the alternative claim of YHWH:

> Have you not known? Have you not heard?
> The Lord is the everlasting God,
> The Creator of the heavens and the earth.
> He does not faint or grow weary,

His understanding is unsearchable.
He gives power to the faint,
and strengthens the powerless. (40:28–29)

I am the Lord, and there is no other;
Besides me there is no god.
I arm you, though you do not know me,
so that they may know, from the rising of the sun
and from the west that there is no one besides me;
I am the Lord, and there is no other.
I form light and create darkness,
I make weal and create woe;
I the Lord do all these things. (45:5–7)

I am God, and there is no other;
I am God, and there is no one like me,
declaring the end from the beginning
and from ancient times things not yet done,
saying, "My purpose shall stand,
and I will fulfill my intent,
calling a bird of prey from the east,
the man for my purpose from a far country.
I have spoken, and I will bring it to pass;
I have planned it, and I will do it. (46:9–11)

I am He; I am the first,
and I am the last.
My hand laid the foundation of the earth,
and my right hand spread out the heavens;
when I summon them,
they stand at attention. (48:12–13)

The "bird of prey, the man for my purpose," is Cyrus the Persian. The stricture is against Babylonian pretense, but the side note is to say that Cyrus, the successor to Babylonia, also is not an autonomous self-starter. He is, even if he does not know it, a tool and a vehicle for the creator God.

It is in that context, I propose, that we are to read the poetry and narrative of Genesis 1–11. These chapters, much of which is appropriated from common Near Eastern liturgical performance, describes a world in which there are pretenders of arrogant autonomy that are juxtaposed to the truth of YHWH as the ultimate source of reality. In asserting the ultimacy of the God of Israel as the creator of the heavens and the earth, these texts assert at the same time the penultimacy and dependence of all other powers, including the pretentions of Babylonia and eventually the claims of Persia as well.

As you know, Genesis 1 opens with a great liturgic fugue that invites our imagination down to the bottom of reality. The mood of the text is not explanatory, but doxological. For that reason, every attempt to use this text in an explanatory way concerning science and religion or creation and evolution is misguided. Its doxological casting serves to voice the self-forgetting wonder in the awesome awareness that the world is evoked by, dependent upon, and accountable to the creator God. As you know from source analysis, the first creation story does not yet give a name to God, not yet YHWH, for the wonder and awe of the creator who is in, with, and under creation is much too overwhelming for specificity.

This liturgical recital sketches out a remembered shalom, remembered before the niceties of historical contestation are even on the screen. That remembered shalom is marked

by an overflow of fruitfulness yielding abundance,
by a declaration of blessing that bestows life-force on
the creation,
by the creation of humankind that is dispatched to
maximize the fruitfulness of the garden of shalom.

Most important, the recital ends in sabbath. The work of creation is, for the creator, demanding work, and God must rest. But God will rest on the seventh day because there is in God, or in God's creation, no restlessness, no anxiety, no disease, and no compulsion to do more. The sabbath day is a festival of well-being that is grounded in divine confidence in the abundance of earth that has been set in motion. The recital of this fugue, participation in this liturgy, participation in the wonder of creation, is to share in that restfulness, and to exult in the abundance.

There can hardly be any doubt that the world sketched here is an alternative to the imperial world of Babylonia or of Persia. Empires, including our own, are premised on scarcity, and therefore on greed, and therefore on violence that wants to extract wealth (taxes in Ezra!) from the colony for the sake of the capital city that never has enough. The capital city, where wealth and power are concentrated and on exhibit, is always a venue for anxiety, for new programs of extraction, and for new muscle by which to coerce extraction. And in the face of that, God rested! God the creator is not a recruit for the empire. God the creator is not a participant in the rat race of scarcity or greed. The bid of the liturgy, moreover, is to invite those who bear this distinctive identity and who have access to this distinctive liturgy to dwell peaceably and well in a blessed, fruitful, and abundant world that regularly culminates in sabbath rest.

This great recital of defiance and alternative is not just a look back. It is a look forward. It is an anticipation of shalom when all the powers of death, the imperial powers of extraction, have been overcome, and there may be rest. The sabbath is an anticipation of a coming governance when God's restfulness will not be disrupted by imperial designs of anxiety, greed, or violence. This prospect, toward which the liturgy moves, is an invitation to its addressees to break free of imperial compulsion to live in sync with the creator God, to trust the abundance. Thus Michael Fishbane, in his exquisite exposition of sabbath, can write:

> A sense of inaction takes over, and the day does not merely mark the stoppage of work or celebrate the completion of creation, but enforces the value that the earth is a gift of divine creativity, given to mankind in sacred trust. . . . To the degree possible, one must also attempt to bring the qualities of inaction and rest into the heart and mind. . . . Observance of the sabbath trains the mind to move from the habitude of action to the ultimate borders of an imaginable immensity, where one can only put oneself in mind of a reality altogether exceeding normal activities and objects.[6]

Such rest of "heart and mind" entails divestment of the hopes and fears that are propelled by the force of scarcity, anxiety, and greed. In a word, it is divestment of the dominating ideology of the empire that always believes that one more act of accumulation or one more accomplishment will make life better. Sabbath is a bodily declaration, grounded in God's own life, that such a way in the world, supervised by empire, is false and deathly.

We find a parallel to Fishbane's eloquent Jewish articulation in the familiar Jewish word of Jesus:

Come to me, all you that are weary and are carrying heavy burdens, and I will give you rest. Take my yoke on you, and learn from me; for I am gentle and humble in heart, and you will find rest for your souls. For my yoke is easy, and my burden is light. (Matt 11:28–29)

The "yoke," which often means the imposition of empire, keeps one weary. The offer of Jesus is to a restfulness that is not only a day, but a way of life premised on abundance.

Shalom Interrupted

But, of course, sabbath can only last until sundown on the seventh day. The text must push on to the eighth day and to the vexations of historical existence. For that reason, the so-called second creation narrative arrives finally at the tree of "knowledge of good and evil," which is of interest to us and to the first couple precisely because it is forbidden (Gen 2:17).

The story is laden with tricky detail and nuance to which attention must be paid. The point I wish to pursue is the appearance of the serpent and the emergence of desire. The narrative strains to show how it is that this remembered shalom was massively interrupted. The intrusion came via a serpent, the most crafty of all creatures. It strikes me as wise for the preacher not to use the language of "fall" or "original sin," terms that are sure to be misunderstood. Much better in my judgment is to let the narrative have its way, that there is a cunning deception in the midst of shalom, that there is a readiness to transgress the divine forbidding, and that what is forbidden is much to be desired. The man and the woman desired to be wise, as wise as the serpent. The term "desire" is the same word we have in the tenth commandment, "covet." It occurs to me that the successive narratives of Genesis 3–11 are regularly about distorted desire that leaves one out of sync with the abundant ordering of creation and with the creator who wills such abundance. Distorted desire becomes the *Leitmotif* for what follows, even though this narrative account leaves much about that desire concealed and unexplained.

It is possible to imagine that the Babylonian and Persian enterprises guaranteed distorted desire, that these empires postured themselves as ultimate and absolute without recognition of any transcendence that was beyond their own claims.

It is possible in the same way to imagine that the US empire of consumerism, with its restless, compulsive advertising, functions to generate distorted desire on which the consumer economy depends.

But after such imperial rootage of distorted desire is acknowledged, the narrative pushes beneath it to say that its force is much more elemental and more intrusive in human life than even imperial imagination. In Christian tradition, Augustine is the great theologian of desire who can see that distorted desire is the taproot of trouble. In that distortion, he says, we come to *use* what we are to love and, conversely, to *love* that which we are to use, and we confuse the practice of relationships with the utilization of commodity. Eventually everything in a world of distorted desire is reduced to commodity, and commodity requires a life of possession, control, and mastery in which practices of fidelity become impossible.

I suggest that Psalm 73 is a primal script for probing desire. In verses 2–14 the psalmist describes a life propelled by greedy envy in which he wants to imitate the arrogant "wicked" who specialize in commodities. Such specialization comes always with abuse of the neighbor and with cynical mocking of the reality of God:

> Therefore pride is their necklace;
> violence covers them like a garment.
> Their eyes swell out with fatness;
> Their hearts overflow with follies.
> They scoff and speak with malice;
> loftily they threaten oppression.
> They set their mouths against heaven,
> and their tongues range over the earth. (vv. 6–9)

But then, in verse 17, the stance of the psalmist is transformed. It is as though, in the sanctuary, the speaker "comes to himself" and recognizes that his true desire, his only desire, is God:

> Whom have I in heaven but you?
> and there is nothing on earth that I desire other than
> you.
> My flesh and my heart may fail,
> but God is the strength of my heart and my portion
> forever. (vv. 25–26)

This is a psalm of recovery in which the speaker moves out of distorted desire and into authentic desire for life with God. Sarah Coakley, I mention in passing, is now parsing the way in which desire for God is a major accent of the Cappadocian Fathers and of course for Augustine who came to recognize the only desire in which his restlessness would end.[7]

Psalm 73 shows a path beyond distorted desire. But, of course, the Genesis text provides no such path. What follows in Genesis 4–11 is working out of distorted desire that eventuates in violence. The speaker of Psalm 73 recognized that a pursuit of distorted desire led inevitably to violence:

> Pride is their necklace;
> *violence* covers them like a garment. (v. 6)

The connection is predictable. Distorted desire requires violence. So in Genesis 4, Cain kills his brother; he had reduced his relationship with God to a contest that he could not win. The premise of the flood narrative is violence in the earth:

> God saw that the earth was filled with *violence*. And God saw that the earth was corrupt; for all flesh had corrupted its ways on the earth. And God said to Noah, "I have determined to make an end to all flesh, for the earth is filled with *violence* because of them. Now I am going to destroy them along with the earth. (Gen 6:11–13)

It is the same term for "violence" as in the psalm. In the narrative of the tower of Babel, moreover, the builders of the city and the tower seek to establish a totalizing regime that inevitably culminates in violent control and mastery. It is in all a tale of violence from chapter 3 through chapter 11. And the violence is not incidental. It is intrinsic to the narrative and I dare say programmatic for the whole.

The sum of these chapters is an invitation to reflect on the seeds of violence in a drama that reduces all things desired to an acquirable commodity. Those seeds of violence, moreover, rooted in an inexplicable temptation, grow strong and defining in the life of the world. The preacher has a chance to reflect on violence, on the way in which our cultural world is premised on and shot through with violence that serves a hunger for self-security that is not on offer. It is insatiable desire that propels such violence. As Helder has seen, there is a spiral of violence that is most often not recognized or acknowledged, often coming first in legal form that then evokes illegal response.[8] Sadly, the God of this text sometimes chooses to advance that spiral.[9]

As is so often the case, more than anyone else Gerhard von Rad saw that in this narrative of alienation enacted as violence, every step is countered by God's will and intent for shalom.[10] Thus the first couple, given their distorted desire, is clothed and protected in their shaming nakedness. Cain, the murderer, is given a protective mark. But it is in the flood narrative that we see most clearly the resolve of God's transformative power. At the outset of the narrative, God is "sorry" and "grieves" that he had made humankind (Gen 6:6–7). Amid the divine resolve to "blot out" failed humanity, the ark of protection for Noah and his family matters decisively. It is an act of rescue. But God knows, in sum, that humanity is helplessly out of sync with the purposes of creation.

> The Lord saw that the wickedness of humankind was great in the earth, and that every inclination of the thoughts of their hearts was only evil continually. (6:5)

It is remarkable that after the flood, when God resolves "never again to curse the ground because of humankind," God nonetheless recognizes:

> The inclination of the human heart is evil from youth. (8:21)

In fact, the flood has changed nothing. Nobody was transformed or converted.

Except God! God has moved from a resolve to "blot out" to a promise to restore and protect. The flood has impinged upon God's heart, and God has a new inclination toward humankind, the very humankind preoccupied with distorted desire. It turns out that this narrative is not only about the history of the world. It is about the history of God's heart that is, amid calamity, turned toward humankind.

It is this same turn that Israel discerned in the exile. The text in Deuteronomy 4 begins with God as "devouring fire." But it ends with this same God now become "a merciful God":

> For the Lord your God is devouring fire, a jealous God. When you have had children and children's children, and become corrupt in the land, if you act corruptly by making an idol in the form of anything, thus doing what is evil in the sight of the Lord your God, and provoking him to anger, . . . you will soon perish from the land that you are crossing the Jordan to occupy. You will not live long on it, but will be utterly destroyed. The Lord will scatter you among the peoples. . . . From there you will seek the Lord your God, and you will find him if you search after him with all your heart and soul. . . . Because the Lord your God is a merciful God, he will neither abandon nor destroy you. He will not forget the covenant with your ancestors that he swore to them. (Deut 4:24–31)

It is the same remarkable divine turn in Isaiah 54:7–8 when divine compassion prevails, but only after displacement and abandonment. First the abandonment:

> For a brief moment I abandoned you; . . .
> In overflowing wrath for a moment I hid my face from
>   you.

But then, in both lines, the divine turn:

But with great compassion I will gather you, . . .
But with everlasting love I will have compassion on
    you,
says the Lord, your Redeemer.

The text goes on to link this divine turn to the flood narrative:

This is like the days of Noah to me:
just as I swore that the waters of Noah
would never again go over the earth;
so I have sworn that I will not be angry with you
and will not rebuke you. (v. 9)

This divine turn is marked in Psalm 103:

He does not deal with us according to our sins,
nor repay us according to our iniquities.
For as the heavens are high above the earth,
so great is his steadfast love toward those who fear him;
as far as the east is from the west,
so far he removes our transgressions from us.
As a father has compassion for his children,
so the Lord has compassion for those who fear him.
For he knows how we are made;
he remembers [from Genesis 2] how we were made;
he remembers that we are dust. (vv. 10–14)

It occurs to me that as the psalmist in Psalm 73 has his heart changed through the course of the psalm, so God, not unlike the psalmist, is moved to newness.[11] The narrative attests that "blotting out" is not God's final verdict; the creator God is fully committed to the remembered shalom of Genesis 1. And so the post-flood covenant is a covenant of fidelity with "every living creature, all flesh that is on the earth" (9:16). The promise is to all, not just to the qualified family of Noah.

In this telling of the history of the world and of the life of God, the tower of Babel story is like the final gasp of the chronicle of violence, an attempt at totalizing control. God breaks up that totalizing effort, as God does every such effort:

> So the Lord scattered them abroad from there over the face of all the earth, and they left off building the city. (11:8)

But beyond the scattering, God does yet one more thing. Around the narrative of the tower in which there is an overreach in hubris, the text provides a continuing genealogy beginning with Shem, one of the sons of Noah. Before the tower narrative, the genealogy had traced the nations from Noah and his three sons, ending with Seth (10:1–32):

> These are the descendants of Shem, by their families, their languages, their lands, and their nations. These are the families of Noah's sons, according to their genealogies in their nations; and from these the nations spread abroad on the earth after the flood. (10:31–32)

Now after the tower narrative, the genealogy is resumed with attention only to the line of Shem. The narrative has made an unacknowledged decision that the future belongs to the line of Shem. Now, in 11:10–26, the narrative culminates with Terah and his sons:

> When Terah had lived seventy years, he became the father of Abram, Nahor, and Haran. (11:26)

The tower narrative did not interrupt the family line. In its unacknowledged preeminence, nonetheless, the genealogy of Shem reeks of chosenness. The genealogy has made a segue from the narrative of violence to the narrative of chosenness that is portrayed as an antidote to the narrative of violence that characterizes the world.

Except, of course, that this sequence ends in an apparent dead end:

Now Sarai was barren; she had no child. (11:30)

Thus the proposal to solve worldly violence by chosenness seems to go nowhere. At first reading, this divine strategy seems as unproductive as were the previous divine attempts at shalom. Up until the end of chapter 11, which marks the culmination of the "history of the world" in Genesis, the contradiction between the narrative of violence that ends in curse and the genealogy of chosenness that offers an alternative to the narrative of violence is left without resolution. In successive episodes, the narrative attests that God will not give in to violence that is rooted in distorted desire. The creator God would not let the skewed desire of the first couple, or the sibling violence of Cain, or the violence of the pre-flood world, or the hubris of the tower win the day. We are left with the will of the creator for a fruitful, blessed creation that is deeply contested.

The preacher has opportunity to bear witness to the restorative will of the creator for blessed shalom. But the preacher also can attest to the contradictory narrative of violence that resists the divine will. It is unfortunate that many preachers have been educated in the precision of source analysis or in tracing Near Eastern mythic parallels as though somehow these critical exposes would deliver to us the "original intent" of this remarkable narrative.

But the preacher knows better. The preacher knows that these thick texts never "meant" in any original way. Rather they always "mean," present tense. They always "mean" in the horizon of ancient Israel in the sixth-century Babylonian exile and in the fifth–fourth centuries of Persian hegemony. They "mean" that the displaced should not succumb to the totalizing narrative of the superpowers but should hold to and honor and recite these narratives that tell the life of the world differently. The decisive difference in this telling is that YHWH, the creator of heaven and earth, is the decisive player, and the totalizing regime that pretends otherwise has it wrong. The narrative of violence that continues to be reperformed even among us is not the last truth of the world. The final truth of the world is the will of the creator God who will go to staggering lengths to counter the narrative of violence rooted in distorted desire that refuses the nonnegotiable shape of the world given by the creator.

The text always "means." And now it "means" among us when the preacher shows that we ourselves are situated in this contradiction between the narrative of violence and the will of the creator. We readers of these texts and our preachers "do" the text amid a narrative that pits the renegade violence of "terrorists/freedom fighters" against the ordered violence of the superpower with its unregulated military power, its ruthless control of markets and resources, its endless surveillance, and its management of cheap labor. In that thick narrative, the "legal" violence of the superpower and its adherents, supported by violent spectator sports, lust for gain, and war on the poor, seems vastly superior to the terrorists/freedom fighters. That narrative of violence permits some violence to appear more moral than other violence, and its practitioners more righteous.

But the text speaks differently to this little sub-community amid the empire. This text summons the little community of faith and attentive listening to resist the dominant narrative of violence, and to hold to and practice an alternative narrative that is occupied by another Character who speaks of blessed fruitfulness against the world of curse. The world of curse is everywhere in the narrative, a condition evoked by distorted desire:

To the serpent:

> Cursed are you among all animals
> And all wild creatures;
> upon your belly you shall go,
> and dust you shall eat all the days of your life.
>   (Gen 3:14)

To the man:

> Cursed is the ground because of you;
> In toil you shall eat of it all the days of your life;
> thorns and thistles it shall bring forth for you,
> and you shall eat the plants of the field.
> By the sweat of your face you shall eat bread
> until you return to the ground,
> for out of it you were taken;
> you are dust, and to dust you shall return. (3:17–19)

To the woman:

> I will greatly increase your pangs in childbearing;
> In pain you shall bring forth children,
> yet your desire shall be for your husband,
> and he shall rule over you. (3:16)

To Cain:

> And now you are cursed from the ground, which has opened its mouth to receive your brother's blood from your hand. When you till the ground, it will no longer yield to you its strength; you will be a fugitive and a wanderer on the earth. (4:11–12)

To Canaan:

> Cursed be Canaan;
> lowest of slaves you shall be to his brothers. (9:22)

And even where the word "curse" is not used, the action tells the same.

The preacher tells this; and then the preacher tells more and other. The preacher tells of the resolve of the flood-causing God:

> I will never again curse the ground because of human-
>   kind . . .
> nor will I ever again destroy every living creature as I
>   have done.
> As long as the earth endures,
> seedtime and harvest, cold and heat,
> summer and winter, day and night
> shall not cease. (8:21–22)

And the prophetic poem extends that divine resolve exactly to the community of exile:

> Just as I swore that the waters of Noah would never
>   again cover the earth,
> so I have sworn that I will not be angry with you
> and will not rebuke you.
> For the mountains may depart

and the hills be removed,
but my steadfast love shall not depart from you,
and my covenant of peace shall not be removed,
says the Lord who has compassion on you.
(Isa 54:9–10)

The community meets to tell otherwise. It meets to resist the "big meeting" that is one of despair. It meets to listen to an alternative narrative. The preacher does not flinch from the truth of violence. Nor does the preacher flinch from an alternative that violates the triumphal mindset of those who settle in despair. The preacher, like the text, commits an epistemological embarrassment and attests that the will for blessing is intrinsic to God's world and cannot be obliterated. Confidence in this alternative resolve is not a generic good idea. It is a narrative-specific resolve declared in divine utterance. It is this God who manages the sweep of violence and who, at the last minute, summons the little community to its pedigree of blessing.

Finally we arrive at Abram and Sarah and barrenness. And there we wait. We wait for divine utterance by this God who is not silenced even by violence. This God has already declared, "I will not again curse the earth because of humankind" (8:21). But that is not enough. We wait for more than divine restraint.

To Be Blessing

The wait is not long. We segue into the ancestral narratives of Abraham and Sarah, Isaac and Rebekkah, Jacob and Rachel, and finally Joseph. We simply turn one page in the text, and there is this utterance that counters the curse. The curse will be defeated by the carriers of blessing, the blessing given by the creator God who first blessed the creatures and then blessed the human creatures. Now God blesses this little community that is to make its way in the Babylonian empire, or in the Persian Empire, or in the Roman Empire, or in the US Empire, to make its way in a career of blessing that refuses the dominant narrative of violence rooted in distorted desire:

> Go from your country and your kindred and your father's house to the land that I will show you. I will make of you a great nation, and I will bless you, and make your name great, so that you will be a blessing. I will bless those who bless you, and the one who curses you I will curse; and in you all the families of the earth shall be blessed. (Gen 12:1–3)

It is all about being chosen as recipient of the blessing of the creator God. But Abraham is not just a recipient of the blessing. He is a carrier, for the blessing extends beyond him to all the families of the earth, that is, to all the peoples who inhabit the narrative of violence in Genesis 3–11. This extraordinary divine commitment revolves around a profound tension that has shown up variously among Jews and Christians; on the one hand it is a wondrous gift and status to be chosen, inviting Abraham's people to bask in a great name and a land. On the other hand, the blessing concerns others. Clearly neither Jews nor Christians have managed this tension well, and there is, I suppose, a subtext of Genesis 12–50 concerning how to negotiate the tension of being both recipient and carrier.

The promise of blessing to others persists in the narrative, as von Rad and Westermann saw.[12] It is uttered three times to Abraham, not only in 12:1–3, but twice more:

> Shall I hide from Abram what I am about to do, seeing that Abram shall become a great and mighty nation, and all the nations of the earth shall be blessed in him? (18:18)

> I will indeed bless you and I will make your offspring as numerous as the stars of heaven and as the sand that is on the seashore. And your offspring shall possess the gate of their enemies, and by your offspring shall all the nations of the earth gain a blessing for themselves, because you have obeyed my voice. (22:17–18)

The blessing is reiterated to Isaac:

> I will make your offspring as numerous as the stars of heaven, and will give to your offspring all these lands; and all the nations of the earth shall gain blessing for themselves through your offspring. (26:4)

The blessing is repeated to Jacob:

> The land on which you lie I will give to you and to your offspring; and your offspring shall be like the dust of the earth, and you shall spread abroad to the west and to the east and to the north and to the south; and all the families of the earth shall be blessed in your and in your offspring. (28:13–14)

The chosen people have a wondrous gift (in German, *Gabe*) and a formidable task (*Aufgabe*). It is remarkable that the promise is not voiced in the Joseph narrative, and scholars are quick to notice that the Joseph narrative in 37–50 is of a quite different genre. As near as the promise comes to speech in the Joseph narrative is a word addressed to father Jacob:

> Do not be afraid to go down to Egypt, for I will make of you a great nation there. I myself will go down with you to Egypt, and I will bring you up again. (46:3–4)

But there is no mention of the blessing for the nations. In sum, however, this little community of Abraham is affirmed in its purpose to be an antidote to the history of violence.

Remarkably, that wondrous promise is carried by a genuinely dysfunctional family:

* Abraham lies about Sarah in order to protect himself (12:10–20).
* Abraham secures a surrogate wife as substitute for barren Sarah (16:2–3).
* Jacob deceives his father, robs his brother, and must run for his life from his brother Esau (27:35).
* Jacob cons his uncle Laban and with Rachel steals the household gods (31:19–21).
* Joseph has brothers who would like to kill him, but who finally deport him into slavery (37:20, 26–28).

This inventory of dysfunction is perhaps echoed in Paul's realism about the church:

> Not many of you were wise by human standards, not many were powerful, not many were of noble birth. But God chose what is foolish in the world to shame the wise. God chose what is weak in the world to shame the strong. God chose what is low and despised in the world, things that are not, to reduce to nothing things that are. (1 Cor 1:26–28)

What preacher does not think, on a low day, that she has in the church the foolish, the weak, and the low and despised who are "not"? The early church, Paul sees, has nothing about which to boast. And long before, the family of Abraham had no bragging rights. But, of course, the tension between the wondrous promise and its shabby carriers is exactly the point, that unlike the superpower people who are strong, young, and beautiful, the little community "from below" relies on less-than-glorious characters, culminating in Christian tradition that can say of Jesus and of his company of followers,

> He has no form or majesty that we should look at him,
> nothing in his appearance that we should desire him.
> He was despised and rejected by others,
> a man of suffering and acquainted with infirmity;
> and as one from whom others hid their faces,
> he was despised, and we held him of no account.
> (Isa 53:2–3)

1. Abraham as a carrier is presented as the quintessential man of faith, preoccupied with the vertical reality of his life. Jon Levenson suggests the way in which the obedience of Genesis 22 and his argument with God in Genesis 18 together attest to the truth and strength of Abraham's faith: on the one hand (Genesis 18) Abraham resisted the intent of God to destroy; on the other hand (Genesis 22) Abraham is readily submissive to God's will.[13] Both resistance and submissiveness are essential in covenantal faith. Faith, in the Abraham tradition, is a demanding engagement that is much more nuanced and complex than the reductionism of "by faith" in Hebrews 11:8–12 might suggest.

2. Isaac gets brief mention in this recital, perhaps included because he was a champion of one segment of this little community of promise. His presence in the narrative, however, serves primarily to exhibit the pathos that marks the history of this family when Esau discovers that he has been betrayed and deceived by his smooth-skinned brother. The vocation of promise-carrier is not all that easy, as the narrative descends into candor about the way in which even this family conducts its life. His narrative ends with loud pathos:

> When Esau heard his father's words, he cried out with an exceedingly great and bitter cry, and he said to his father, "Bless me, me also, father!" But he said, "Your brother came deceitfully, and he has taken away your blessing." Esau said, "Is he not rightly named Jacob? For he has supplanted me these two times. He has taken away my birthright; and look, now he has taken away my blessing." Then he said, "Have you not reserved a blessing for me?" Isaac answered Esau, "I have already made him your lord, and I have given him all his brothers as servants, and with grain and wine I have sustained him. What then can I do for you, my son?" Esau said to his father, "Have you only one blessing, father? Bless me, me also, father!" And Esau lifted his voice and wept. (27:34–38)

Before he is finished, Isaac will speak a blessing, blessing his older son Esau who had lost his birthright (27:39–40).

The preacher knows and can watch the beloved community come forward to receive the Eucharist. The preacher, being a pastor as well, knows the cry that each one carries, including those who voice no cry. The cry is about being left out because you sense that someone else has the blessing that belongs right-fully to you. It is no wonder that Esau lifted up his voice and wept. He did so for the whole family! Transmission of the blessing to the next generation, as every congregation knows, is never an easy process. It often entails pathos, loss, displacement, and durable alienation.

3. Jacob the fugitive manages to usurp the blessing and manages to transmit it to his grandsons. What a career in deception he performs, though nowhere does the narrative commit a reprimand for Jacob for his conduct; even by the norms of this family, he is a performer of distorted desire. He is a conniver, driven by his fear and by his lust for having it all. In most interpretation, the narrative is seen to pivot on that enigmatic dream narrative in chapter 32 (vv. 22–32). Jacob is, for good reason, fearful for his life while he is awake. And then, when he is asleep, he finds his life deeply contested. Like many nightmares, the characters in this dream are not clearly identified. He wrestled, we are told, "with a man" (v. 24). But he got a blessing, seemingly from God. Indeed, he said, "I have seen God face to face" (v. 30). The matter is not clear: "you have striven with God and with man" (v. 28). Well, maybe it was God; maybe it was a man; maybe it was his brother Esau who must have haunted him. Maybe it was both of them, or all of them, or any of them. It was a nightmare that came upon the chosen. And even his restorative interaction with his brother ends with one more deception.

> Let my lord pass on ahead of his servant, and I will lead on slowly, according to the pace of the cattle that are before me and according to the pace of the children, until I come to my lord in Seir. (33:14)

But the narrative ends laconically:

> But Jacob journeyed to Succoth, and built himself a
> house, and made booths for his cattle; therefore the
> place is called Succoth. (v. 17)

He went the other way! He never intended to meet his brother
again, at least not until they had together buried their father
(35:29). At the end of this narrative, God blessed Jacob yet
once more:

> Your name is Jacob; no longer shall you be called Jacob,
> but Israel shall be your name. . . . I am God Almighty;
> be fruitful and multiply; a nation and a company of
> nations shall come from you, and kings shall spring
> from you. The land that I gave to Abraham and Isaac
> I will give to you, and I will give the land to your off-
> spring after you. (35:9–12)

The land promise is intact. But the promise concerning the
nations has dropped out, as though no longer remembered.

4. Joseph, narrated in a different genre, serves as travel music
to transport Israel from Canaan to Egypt. He is never inducted
into the promise. And while we like, in our happy exposition,
to celebrate his performance of God's providence in feeding his
brothers amid famine, in fact the narrative ends otherwise. Right
from his arrival in Egypt, he begins to play the Egyptian game,
to participate, seemingly with an unbothered conscience, in the
Egyptian narrative of violence (39:1–6). Already in chapter 41,
he has become second in the empire, second only to Pharaoh:

> "You shall be over my house, and all my people shall
> order their lives at your command; only with regard

to the throne will I be greater than you. . . . See, I have set you over all the land of Egypt." Removing his signet ring from his hand, Pharaoh put it on Joseph's hand; he arrayed him in garments of fine linen, and put a gold chain around his neck. He had him ride in the chariot of his second-in-command; and they cried out in front of him, "Bow the knee!" Thus he set him over all the land of Egypt. Moreover Pharaoh said to Joseph, "I am Pharaoh, and without your consent no one shall lift up hand or foot in all the land of Egypt." (41:40–44)

It is as though Joseph has traded his family identity of promise for life in Pharaoh's court. It does happen; folks forget the narrative. Carriers of the promise compromise and then sell out. By the end of the narrative, we are told that Joseph, as Pharaoh's food czar, has bargained with hungry peasants to give them Pharonic food (that turned out to be the "bread of affliction") in exchange for their cattle, their land, and finally their bodies (47:13–26). He pushes the peasants out of the economy and reduces them to slavery.

We often begin reading the book of Exodus with God's people in slavery. We do not, however, often enough reflect on how they got there. They got there, we are now told, because one of the members of the sub-community forgot the mandate of blessing, capitulated to the dominant narrative, and became Pharaoh's agent in economic "development" that resulted in enslavement. They ended in slavery, as often happens with the enormous leverage of concentrations of wealth and power in the hands of the few at the expense of the hungry many. It is not a surprise that Leon Kass can read the Joseph narrative as "the Egyptianization of Joseph" as a full participant in the narrative of violence.[14] It is astonishing, in retrospect, that the divine promise has been so resilient, no thanks to some of its carriers who trade the promise for distorted desire.

Father Jacob has not yet finished with his puckish tricks. The old man is to bless his grandsons, Ephraim and Manasseh, or as they were until that moment, Manasseh and Ephraim. Jacob blesses his son Joseph one more time:

> May the God before whom my fathers Abraham and Isaac walked . . . bless the boys; and in them let my name be perpetuated, and the name of my fathers Abraham and Isaac; and let them grow to a multitude on the earth. (48:15–16)

Then Jacob blesses the grandsons. He crosses hands, so that his right hand of power is on the head of Ephraim, the younger (48:14). Joseph protests the cross (48:17). He had a clear sense of order and propriety, inured as he was to Pharonic kinds of entitlement. But the old man would not be corrected. He said to his son concerning his grandsons:

> I know, my son, I know; he also shall become a people, and he also shall be great. Nevertheless his younger brother shall be greater than he, and his offspring shall become a multitude of nations. (48:19)

Jacob knew, from his own shabby experience, that the force of promise does not operate according to established rules and protocols. There is something subversive and quixotic about the promise that will not be domesticated or restrained. So he blessed the grandsons as he proposed to do:

By you Israel will invoke blessings, saying,
God make you like Ephraim and like Manasseh. (v. 20)

The narrative of promise that means to subvert the curse of the world is raw, disordered, awkward, and needs a good editing. But then, it would be like that, because editors tend to work with the "big story." As Freud understood about the subversive alternative, it is raw, disordered, and awkward. But it has force, authority, and effect. And the preacher is to let the force, authority, and effect be available so that the faithful may be aware that we are situated in an alternative narrative that refuses, as we are able, the distorted desires of the world that always puts our tradition at risk. The ancestral stories, particular, peculiar, and problematic as they are, keep insisting, "Don't forget, don't give up, don't capitulate."

What chance does a promise have in a world of violence? Well, not much. But it is our birthright and it is our preaching task. It strikes me that Luke the evangelist knew this. He has mother Mary sing of the revolution her child of promise would perform:

He has brought down the powerful from their thrones,
and lifted up the lowly;
he has fed the hungry with good things,
and sent the rich away empty. (Luke 1:52–53)

And then Mary concludes:

He has helped his servant Israel,
in remembrance of his mercy,
according to the promise he made to our ancestors,
to Abraham and to his descendants forever. (vv. 54–55)

It is according to the promise to Abraham—forever! And Jesus summons people to participate in this alternative narrative. To the woman crippled for eighteen years, he says:

> And ought not this woman, a *daughter of Abraham* whom Satan bound for eighteen long years, be set free from this bondage on the sabbath day? (Luke 13:16)

To Zacchaeus, the despised revenue officer, he says,

> Today salvation has come to this house, because he too is a *son of Abraham.* (Luke 19:9)

In his parable concerning the rich man and the poor man, Lazarus, it is the poor man who is carried away by the angels to be *with Abraham* (Luke 16:22).

We live in a narrative of distorted desire that is urged by malevolent forces. It is the conviction of the preacher and the hope of the church that there is a better narrative, "a more excellent way" that offers desire that is congruent with the reality of God. The true story is the narrative of blessing. It is carried by a frail, conflicted people. Under good preaching, we are always again invited into the counter narrative that refuses the death sentence that we love too much.

The book of Genesis is beforehand. It is before the Exodus and before the emergence of Jesus. It is the narrative that Paul can dub "the gospel beforehand" (Gal 3:8). The preacher will have done well to show us the concrete ways in which we are situated between the narrative of violence and the counter narrative of welcome. We have these compromised models in the ancestral stories; they are resonant with our own ambiguity. We do well to cross our hands when we bless, thus defying the usual protocols of control.

2

Preaching from the Torah:
The Tale of Moses

I call it the Moses "Tale" because historical questions on this text are acute. We do not know about its "historicity." What we know, and have always known when we pay attention, is that it rings true paradigmatically.[1] Whenever it may have happened, it keeps happening. The task of the preacher is to assure that it happens now yet again, that it happens in a credible performance, both as a scathing critique and as a buoyant possibility. The church needs to see the tale in all its dramatic force. It is the preacher's luxury to linger over each segment of the text, to tell the entire tale through the lens of little text. For the whole of the tale is a little text that witnesses against the big text of Pharaoh.

Profiling Pharaoh

The preacher and the congregation must have in purview the totalizing propensity of Pharaoh.[2] What we get with Moses is

Pharaoh's narrative told "from below" by his adversaries and victims.

We see Pharaoh first in Genesis 12:10–20. We learn two things about him. First he had, due to the Nile, the world's most reliable food supply, the place to go in a famine. Second, we see his propensity for confiscating, for his advisers had to be procurement agents to get yet other beautiful women for him, in this case our "princess," Sarah. His propensity from the outset is to have everything and to want still more.

But this powerful man who has everything and wants more is beset by nightmares of scarcity (Gen 41:1–7). In the night when his guard is down, he is beset by anxiety so vivid and so dramatic that his intelligence community is unable to decipher it for him. He dreams, in his anxiety over not having enough, of seven cows that devour seven cows, and seven shocks of grain that devour seven shocks of grain. He dreams of devouring and being devoured.

Given the failure of his intelligence community, he finally must find a Hebrew, albeit a Hebrew prisoner, who can decode his nightmares. In a long anticipation of Freud, Pharaoh already discerns that this Hebrew community is able to live a double life of public performance and secret discernment, secrets hidden from Pharaoh and his intelligence officers. Joseph, the one who can discern beyond the ken of the Egyptians, not only knows the nightmare. Beyond that, he is willing and able to be a house advisor to Pharaoh. Indeed, he is ready—who would not be?—to be co-opted as the food czar to secure even more for this mega-force that already has more than enough. Such a mega-force of superpower can always recruit locals who will be willing agents for more accumulation.

Now we have this Hebrew acting on behalf of this onerous, confiscatory propensity of Pharaoh who already had enough and more. In a remarkable text, the Hebrew food czar colludes with the mega-force to turn accumulation into monopoly, all powered by anxiety (Gen 47:13–26). The peasants, the cheap labor force, need food in famine; Joseph sells food to them from Pharaoh's accumulation. In the second year of the famine, the peasants need more food, but now they have no money with which to buy food. Joseph takes their cattle in exchange for food. He seizes their means of production and puts them out of business. In the third year of the famine, without money and without cattle and without tradable goods, they still need food. It does not occur to this Hebrew food czar, acting on behalf of Pharaoh, to give them food, for in Pharaoh's domain there is no free lunch. Because they are hungry, they trade away their bodies and their land:

> Buy us and our land in exchange for food. Just give us seed, so that we may live and not die, and that the land may not become desolate. (Gen 47:19)

Because of Pharaoh's propensity to accumulate, his accumulation, in the hands of Joseph, becomes a monopoly that leads to enslavement. The process has been an obvious one that exhibits the full import of Pharaoh's confiscatory policy. It could not have ended in any other way except monopoly.

This is, however, more than monopoly. This is a totalism to which the peasants-become-slaves gladly conform:

> You have saved our lives; may it please my lord, we will be slaves to Pharaoh. (v. 25)

43

The peasants do not make a sound about the coercive policies of Pharaoh; instead they express gratitude to Pharaoh. The deference shown to Pharaoh merits attention. Pharaoh now has more than a monopoly of food. He has a monopoly of imagination in which the peasants-become-slaves cannot imagine themselves except in the domain of Pharaoh where they have become helpless performers of cheap labor. Pharaoh's relentless claim propelled by anxiety about scarcity eventuates in accumulation become monopoly. That is Pharaoh's story. The one with the most is propelled by the most intense anxiety to the hurt of others. Pharaoh has now achieved total control of land, bodies, technology, and imagination. All the others must conform and Joseph, now completely "Egyptianized," has made it all possible![3]

The preacher's task, I propose, is to tell this part of the story in order to equip the church to do social analysis about the propensity to accumulation that ushers in an ideological totalism that will not permit any initiative for life outside the sphere of the governance of the regime. Such a totalizing propensity or course can turn up anywhere, to which we ourselves are witnesses. It can turn up as:

* a relentless theological orthodoxy that excludes and excommunicates;
* a moral code that is inhospitable to nuance;
* an economic system that specializes in accumulative greed; or
* a media monopoly that suppresses what is unwelcome.

The Pharonic sequence of scarcity-anxiety-accumulation-monopoly goes one cubit further.

It is in my Bible exactly three pages from Genesis 47 to Exodus 1. The peasant population reduced to slavery may be different from one text to the other. All it takes to connect them is "a new king" who does not honor the old promises. The new king simply extends the confiscatory policies of the old king, now even to the Hebrews. And by the second paragraph of Exodus, we are told:

> The Egyptians became ruthless in imposing tasks on the Israelites, and made their lives bitter with hard service in mortar and brick and in every kind of field labor. They were ruthless in all the tasks that they imposed on them. (Exod 1:13–14)

It is no surprise that the confiscatory policies of Pharaoh ended in violence. Well, how could they not? Once the regime—hard orthodoxy, intolerant morality, an economy of accumulation, media monopoly—established its ideological totalism, there are no restrains or limits. Totalism, in its many forms, is free to enact violence among the vulnerable and powerless, to exclude them from the monopoly of riches, and to label them as disqualified and unworthy.[4] The disqualification is already apparent in Genesis 43:32:

> They served him [Joseph] by himself, and them by themselves, and the Egyptians who ate with him by themselves, because the Egyptians could not eat with the Hebrews, for that is an abomination to the Egyptians.

It is put in more direct terms in Exodus 5:21:

> You have brought us into bad odor with Pharaoh and his officials, and have put a sword into their hand to kill us.

The Hebrews were in a "bad odor" with the Egyptians, disqualified. It could not end any other way. It is the preacher's task to help us imagine such a process of adversarial exclusion as the "collateral damage" of accumulation. And then to notice that this is no ancient story but one performed in our very midst, in which we may play various roles as Pharaoh, as Joseph, or as a carrier of a "bad odor."

Totalism Interrupted

Given social analysis about the face of totalism, the story concerns the unexpected interruption of this totalism. Every totalizing regime is characteristically surprised and shocked by interruption. Who knew? Who knew that there were alternatives? Who knew that they were unhappy with the totalism? Who knew there was enough energy or courage or imagination that had not been domesticated to conformity? But of course that is the plotline entrusted to the preacher, that the pharaonic propensity can and has been and will be interrupted.

The interruption is the performance of the gospel. That performance of interruption, however, is not high-minded spirituality. It is tough bodily engagement that contests the all-comprehending power of totalism. The interest of the narrative, and of the preacher's rendering of the narrative, is not just to remember an ancient interruption. It is to energize for and to evoke courage for a contemporary interruption of the violent, lethal totalism that besets us. You will see why I have opened with Pharaoh. It is impossible to think about or imagine *an interruption* without first narrating *the totalism* that is to be interrupted. The hard part is that those of us who dwell in and benefit from the pharaonic arrangement most often do not notice. More than not notice, we resist noticing, because such notice brings with it risky obligation. Thus we may be instructed by that ancient interruption that we may continue to perform.

At the very outset Pharaoh's world is placed in jeopardy by two below-the-radar midwives who refuse to obey Pharaoh's brutal command (Exod 1:15–22). Their brief paragraph attests that the force for life is with the slave community that will "multiply and grow exceedingly strong" (1:7). Beyond that unspoken claim, their action is one of defiance that causes Pharaoh to become even more outrageous in the maintenance of his monopoly. I am not sure that the gender role here is crucial. But clearly in a patriarchal society, that they are unnoticed, uncredentialed women is not unimportant. The tradition knows and remembers their names as the first interrupters. Such an acknowledgment of their names is a dramatic contrast to the nameless Pharaoh. The community of interruption names and remembers those whom the big house dismisses and treats with contempt.

The second interruption is the violent action of Moses when he, in indignation, kills an Egyptian manager of forced labor (2:11–15). Whether this is a calculated or an emotive action against Pharaoh, either way it is a death sentence for Moses as Pharaoh "sought to kill him." The empire must protect its own and cannot permit such an interruption to go unpunished. Those who challenge the monopoly are sure to be marked men and women. Of course it is a great awkwardness for us that this interruption takes the form of violence. The report in any case protects us from any romantic innocence about disrupting Pharaoh's power arrangement. Pharaoh will not yield to sweet talk; there will, perforce, be abrasion. Better it be nonviolent, but abrasion in any case. The action of Moses is quite a contrast to the surreptitious work of the midwives. But they are of a piece. Both Moses and the midwives refuse the claim that pharaonic authority is a given beyond challenge. The entire narrative of interruption is based on the conviction that Pharaoh's regime is not a given, but a construct that can be deconstructed. The first task of the preacher is to subvert the notion that present monopolies are absolute givens.

The third interruption, in the wake of Moses and the midwives, is the public voicing of pain by the slave community, and its evocation of YHWH:

> After a long time the king of Egypt died. The Israelites groaned under their slavery, and cried out. Out of the slavery their cry for help rose up to God. God heard their groaning, and God remembered his covenant with Abraham, Isaac, and Jacob. God looked upon the Israelites, and God took notice of them. (2:23–25)

The breaking of the silence of totalism happened at the change of regime when the king died. When such a king dies, everything becomes unglued, and many things become imaginable. This is not the first moment of pain. The pain of oppression had been there forever. And Pharaoh did not care, as long as it was silent pain. This is not a new discovery or awareness of pain by the slaves. What is new is the voice that breaks silence.[5] The voice from below declares that Pharaoh's monopoly is coming to an end. That voice that insists on sounding and being heard is a revolutionary praxis in which pain now becomes a social fact that all must face.[6] It is a risky act, because the great silencer will react. But silencers are ineffective when the cry is validated by suffering; the cry turns suffering into imaginative energy. The preacher's task is to bring the pain to speech in ways that interrupt all business as usual.

Only then, only after the midwives and Moses and the cry, does YHWH appear in the narrative (Exod 3:1–9). We are in the third chapter of this narrative of emancipation which thus far has been sustained by human insistence. It is as though the Holy One has waited, or has not noticed until now. As Pharaoh is interrupted, so perhaps these initial moves have interrupted YHWH's reverie of indifference. Now there will be no divine indifference. Human pain brought to speech evokes holy power!

Moses, now a fugitive, "turned aside." He heard a voice; he was called by name. The one who speaks occupies holy ground, is identified with the Genesis promises, and now is identified with and will make Israel's future outside the totalism of Pharaoh. This is no ordinary tale. This a tale of the Holy God of promise who stands as alternative to Pharaoh. YHWH (for that is his name) is the big interrupter. We get a series of promises, divine resolve addressed to Moses:

> I have observed the misery of my people who are in Egypt. I have heard their cry on account of their taskmasters. Indeed, I know their suffering, and I have come down to deliver them from the Egyptians, and to bring them up out of that land to a good and broad land, a land flowing with milk and honey. . . . I have seen how the Egyptians oppress them. (3:7–9)

But then, abruptly, the promises turn to mandate:

> I will send you to Pharaoh to bring my people, the Israelites, out of Egypt. (v. 10)

And that leads us to the fifth element of interruption, namely, the mobilization of human agency to act out divine resolve. Moses has been a terrorist or a freedom fighter. But now he is an agent in his own history, an actor in the future of his people. YHWH will not go to Pharaoh. Moses must go to Pharaoh. The devolution of the task from divine resolve to human agency is a defining moment for the preacher. The preacher must eventually turn from God-talk to human talk concerning summons, responsibility, vocation, and risk.

The narrator has arranged the drama that is to be performed and reperformed. It is a drama between *a determined absolutizing totalism* and a *resolve of interruption* powered by *holy promise* and enacted by *human agency*. The meat of the drama is the extended contest, the "plague cycle," that consists in ten performances of conflict that build and build to the denouement (Exod 7:1–12:32). The narrative is not really about frogs or gnats or hail or any of the pyro-theatrics. It is about the relative power of Pharaoh and YHWH, about the waning and defeat of Pharaoh's power, and about the truth of YHWH's resolve. The preaching task is to exhibit the way in which this drama is currently staged among us on the big public screen, the contest of power from above and power from below. The preaching task, moreover, is to give access to that same contest within each of us, the desire to stay the course and the yearning to break to God's freedom, our decision on whether to go or to stay, to conform or to risk.[7] The story told here and by the preacher concerns those who have decided to leave, to trust the interruption, and to notice that the totalism is flawed and phony. By the time he finishes, Moses, the great human interrupter, will exult over the failure of Pharaoh:

Pharaoh's chariots and his army he cast into the sea;
His picked forces were sunk in the Red Sea.
The floods covered them; they went down into the
    depths like a stone. . . .
You blew with your wind, the sea covered them;
They sank like lead in the mighty waters. (15:4–5, 10)

And then, as capstone to elation, Miriam, the other sisters, and the tambourines turned the groans of Israel to a dance of freedom:

Sing to YHWH, for he has triumphed gloriously;
Horse and rider he has thrown into the sea. (v. 21)

The interruption has succeeded!

The Risky Terrain of Departure and Discipleship

But of course the success of the departure is tenuous. Because outside of Pharaoh's domain there is only wilderness, a zone without police regulation or reliable agriculture, without the guarantees of a viable life-support system. The first shock of wilderness— outside Pharaoh's domain—only confirmed Pharaoh's claim that there is nothing outside "my domain." No wonder they immediately wanted to do back—back to safe food, back to sure jobs, back to slavery, back to the totalizing that locked people in and precluded any alternative future (Exod 16:3). The preacher's task is to be honest about the risky terrain of departure and discipleship. And then to tell this amazing story of flourishing life given outside of Pharaoh's totalism. It is inexplicable and unexpected. It turns out—and continues to turn out—that those who depart the totalism are surprised by gifts. They are not easy gifts. Nor are they easily received. The post-Egypt narrative of Exodus 16–17 is about contentious quarreling, about risk and fear and unhappiness with Mosaic leadership, and with the God of the wilderness. They were surprised, when they finally got their eyes off Egypt and turned to face their new arena of risk, that the glory of God was before them (16:10). The wilderness was God-occupied territory, an occupation that changed everything. The old contest had been between Egypt and the God of departure. The new contest is between the God who occupies the wilderness and the yearning to go back. In their fear after departure—to which the preacher gives voice—they stated their needs. They needed bread. It was given, but inscrutably:

> When the layer of dew lifted, there on the surface of the wilderness was a fine flaky substance, as fine as frost on the ground. When the Israelites saw it, they said to one another, "What is it?" (vv. 14–15)

Enough for all, no scarcity as in Egypt:

> The Israelites did so, some gathering more, some less. But when they measured it with an omer, those who gathered much had nothing over, and those who gathered little had no shortage; they gathered as much as each of them needed. (vv.17–18)

They needed meat. They got it in one quick verse:

> In the evening quails came and covered the camp. (v. 13)

It was a gift; but without comment. They needed water. They got it from a rock:

"Strike the rock, and water will come out of it, so that the people may drink." Moses did so in the sight of the elders of Israel. (17:6)

But it was a notorious place of contention.

The supply of bread, meat, and water constituted an amazing wonder for Israel. The wilderness is a place of abundance. It is the abundance of the wilderness that Jesus performed with five thousand and then with four thousand, also in the wilderness (Mark 6:30–44; 8:1–10). The abundance in the wilderness with surpluses left over is a contrast to the nightmarish scarcity of Pharaoh. Pharaoh always accumulated, because he feared scarcity. And the more he accumulated, the more he feared scarcity. He arrived at monopoly, and in his monopoly he was totally afraid. The drama is counterintuitive. We would have thought:

Egypt as a place of abundance;
Wilderness as a place of scarcity.

It is, however, to the contrary:

Egypt is a place of scarcity;
Wilderness is a place of abundance.

It is contrary to expectation, because Pharaoh, unlike YHWH, cannot produce flourishing. It is not in his power to give life abundant. Israel learned that the only abundant life is received when Pharaoh is departed.

Covenant: The Big Divine "If"

And then they came to Sinai. They arrived there and were met immediately by the big divine "if":

If you obey my voice and keep my covenant, you shall
be my treasured possession out of all the peoples.
(Exod 19:5)

They now have a chance—these ex-slaves—to be YHWH's special treasure among all the peoples of the earth. The Exodus initiative of YHWH had been unconditional. But now, for the long
term, the condition is,

Obey my voice;
Keep my covenant.

The "obey," moreover, is an intensive in the form of an absolute infinitive. Really listen!! They had been delivered from the
unjust requirements of Pharaoh. But now they come to what
David Brooks has called "a long obedience." He writes of the
way in which the US founders appealed to the Exodus tradition:

When [the US founders] wanted to put Moses as a
central figure on the Great Seal of the United States,
they were not celebrating him as a liberator, but as a
re-binder. It wasn't just that he had led the Israelites out
of one set of unjust laws. It was that he re-bound them
with another set of laws. Liberating to freedom is the
easy part. Re-binding with just order and accepted compulsion is the hard part.[8]

They were free of Pharaoh; but they were not free. They now
faced new duties and obligations. They signed on immediately!
Long before they were given the commandments, they agreed
to them:

Everything that the Lord has spoken we will do. (19:8)

They agreed before they knew what was to be required. They must have recognized that whatever the Lord of freedom commands, it will be better than the commands of Pharaoh. The claim of Pharaoh was endlessly "make more bricks." Be more productive! In our own society, Pharaoh's command has morphed into consumption: consume more, buy more, own more, eat more, enjoy more, shop more! It is our duty!

The response of 19:8 indicates a readiness, surely a knowing readiness, to trade duties, to stop obedience to Pharaoh and to have the lighter burden and easier yoke of Sinai. The preacher's task is to invite folk into the process of trading duties. Not adding duties. Not continuing obedience to Pharaoh while adding gospel requirements. Rather they relinquish the commands of Pharaoh, who is owed no allegiance, and so obey only the emancipator. I have come to think that the Sinai commands exactly counter Pharaoh.[9] But they cannot be understood in that way unless the preacher does serious social analysis of the way in which the paradigm of Pharaoh continues to be operative among us. Thus as counter-Pharaoh:

The first commandment, "no other gods before me," is an assertion that Israel will not and must not give allegiance to other than YHWH, no more allegiance to the claim of Pharaoh and his requirements. The gods of Egypt are mentioned in the narrative only once (Exod 12:12). But they are everywhere legitimators of a usurpatious economic system. No allegiance to these gods means no commitment to endless productivity and consumption.

The sweeping exclusionary claim of YHWH could of course suggest that YHWH is as totalizing as is Pharaoh. No doubt true. But the defining difference is that the claims of YHWH that allow no compromise are marked by an intense neighborliness that recharacterizes absolutism in terms of the common good. Thus the God of this alternative totalism is the one "who brought you out of Egypt." The exodus is clearly in the purview of the God who commands at Sinai. When the exclusive claim of YHWH is understood to be like that of Pharaoh, the first commandment will have been misunderstood, a misunderstanding that recurs in much authoritarian faith. The first commandment is a genuine alternative to the totalism of Pharaoh.

The second commandment, "no graven images," is a warning, among other things against commodity fetishism that invests ultimate meaning in material objects and credits them with transcendent value. Pharaoh, in his drive to accumulation, is a precursor of all commodity fetishism that believes that ultimate value is in possession, ownership, and control of material goods. Or as the prophet Isaiah has it, it is to "bow down and worship the works of our hands." The commandment characterizes YHWH as a jealous God who will not share authority with Pharaoh and the lords of accumulation. But this God of Sinai is one who is capable of "steadfast love," of tenacious covenantal loyalty, precisely the kind of durable fidelity for which Pharaoh has no capacity at all. Thus the commandment offers a contrast between overvaluing commodity (worshiping the works of our hands) and durable fidelity as the ground for life in the world. Sinai, as the preacher will demonstrate, is the arena of contestation and decision for durable fidelity over the overvaluing of commodity.

The fourth commandment on sabbath, before it had to do with worship, concerned work stoppage. Sabbath is the regular, disciplined, highly visible decision to stop work so that one's existence is not driven by production or by the commodities that are produced. The exodus version of the commandment appeals to the seventh-day rest for the creator. That allusion not only situates sabbath practice in the structure of creation, but tacitly asserts that YHWH, the creator God of rest, is unlike the confiscatory gods of Egypt who can order their little totalism, but cannot and do not deliver the abundant order of creation.

It is clear that there could be no sabbath work stoppage in Pharaoh's domain, not for the slaves, not for the taskmasters, not for the supervisors, not even for Pharaoh. The domain of Pharaoh is an endless rat race with a drive toward monopoly that defined the life of all parties.

In the face of this inevitably exploitative system that necessarily treated workers as dispensable objects, work stoppage is not only an act of resistance, but a mighty alternative in which there is a valuing of more than the meeting of the next quota.[10] The preacher has a chance to bear witness to a life of flourishing that is not propelled by the endless requirements of electronic connectedness in the interest of control.

The terse commands concerning killing, adultery, stealing, and false witness all attest to a different kind of community in which others in the community are ends and not means, not threats to be killed, not objects to be exploited, not victims of theft through laws of credit, interest, and mortgage, not victims of mendacity that generate false social facts.

And of course the capstone of the big ten is "Thou shalt not covet." This commandment does not concern petty impulses to envy. It concerns acquisitiveness, the drive to seize what belongs to another. We now live in a society in which the label "taker" is regularly applied to those who depend on public support. The real "takers" in the purview of the prohibition, however, are those who extract from the common good, who seek always more (like Pharaoh) and are propelled by a drive to possess, occupy, and own well beyond what is needed. It is remarkable that this brief tenth prohibition contains the word "neighbor" three times: neighbor's wife (in a patriarchal society), neighbor's house, and anything that belongs to the neighbor.

This culmination of the Decalogue has to do with an acquisitive economy, exactly the economy of Pharaoh who seized the bodies and lands of the vulnerable and reduced them to slavery. It is clear that the term "neighbor" is one that did not occur in Pharaoh's lexicon. "Neighbor" refers to those who share companionship in a common good; there was no common good in Pharaoh's world, only a stratified arrangement of control and exploitation.

Thus the duties of Sinai, for which Israel traded off obligations to Pharaoh, concern organizing social power and social relations in the community for the common good. Such an organization of social power would have been strange and inimical to Pharaoh, even as it is strange and inimical to our market driven society. It is the preacher's happy opportunity to teach and declare that a different sense of obligation is on offer. David Brooks speaks of this in contemporary mode:

> But Exodus is a reminder that statecraft is soulcraft, that good laws nurture better people. . . . The laws build community by anchoring belief in common practices. The laws moderate religious zeal; faith is not expressed in fiery acts but in everyday habits. The laws moderate the pleasers; they create guardrails that are meant to restrain people from going off to emotional or sensual extremes.[11]

I am struck by how the tale of Moses manages to keep the main themes in tension. There is no doubt that the story of emancipation (chapters 1–15) is linked to the ritual of trading duties (chapters 19–24). It is, moreover, evident that the narrative of abundance (16–17) is in purview as the exodus and Sinai texts are given. The commands of Sinai are in the wake of divine abundance. The Decalogue might have begun:

> I am YHWH who caused you to flourish in the wilderness with bread, meat, and water.

Sinai is a vision of flourishing, of relying on the gifts of the creator rather than the protocols of oppression. The preacher's task is to create an environment in which this extraordinary choice is available. Israel is always rechoosing, again. Without the preacher, such a possibility of companionship in the common good is hardly visible in an economy of accumulation and commodification. Sinai attests that in the end, by the tenth commandment, the project of faithful life is not one of accumulation, but one of neighborliness.

No Cheap or Easy Covenant

The covenant is solemnly sealed with Israel's oath of obedience (24:3, 7). The deal is consummated and Pharaoh is rejected. But of course the process of excluding Pharaoh and his influence remained unfinished business; Pharaoh keeps seeking a return to power with his seductive attractiveness. The narrative of Exodus 24 leaves Moses in the clouds of Sinai. It then rushes to chapter 32; it took the Israelites only ten minutes or so to adjust to Moses's prolonged absence from them. Aaron, his brother and rival, accommodated the anxiety of Israel with a commodity-god, a calf of gold or perhaps a bull of gold. The bull/calf indicates an accent on manly fertility. The gold brings us back to commodity. The combo of bull/gold, of manly fertility and commodity, a combo that is an icon at Wall Street, is a deep departure from neighborly covenantalism. It is, *mutatis mutandis*, a return to Pharaoh's system of values that places accent on accumulated commodity and manly productivity. It is not the same, but it is close enough. Aaron introduces this new homemade god:

> These are your gods, O Israel, who brought you out of the land of Egypt! (32:4)

He credits this god with the exodus, a clear misrepresentation of the exodus narrative and of the exodus God. Deliverance from Pharaoh's totalism was not by manly fertility or by commodity, or by a combination of them, but by the God of emancipatory fidelity.

What follows in Exodus 32–34 is a complex negotiation between YHWH and Moses, after the fracture, to determine what if any future Israel might still have.

At the outset YHWH is angry with Aaron and Israel. Moses is cool with the affront they have committed and manages to talk YHWH down from his angry intention. Except that soon Moses becomes as angry as is YHWH. The outcome is a slaughter and the brokenness of covenant. Clearly the maintenance of an alternative to Pharaoh is hard business; it requires discipline and steadfastness, and includes harsh sanctions of enforcement against violators.

And even after the severe punishment, an alienation remains. It is not clear how to proceed. YHWH and Moses must engage in hard-argued negotiation in which Moses daringly gets in the face of the God of covenant. YHWH assures Moses of YHWH's continuing presence with him:

> "My presence will go with you and I will give you rest."
> (33:14)

But the "you" is singular, you Moses, without mention of Israel. It is Moses, in his rejoinder to YHWH, not YHWH, who mentions "your people."

> "For how shall it be known that I have found favor in your sight, I and your people, unless you go with us? In this way, we shall be distinct, I and your people, from every people on the face of the earth." (33:16)

Moses prizes "your people" more than does YHWH and wants to assure a viable continuation for Israel. That continuation requires that Moses must be in YHWH's face, even as YHWH's face goes before them. In the negotiation that follows,

∗ YHWH promises to go with them to assure Israel's distinctiveness among the peoples (v. 17).
∗ Moses presses the point and wants to see YHWH's glory (v. 18).
∗ YHWH grants Moses access to YHWH's goodness and name, but refuses his request for access to divine glory (v. 19).

And then YHWH asserts YHWH's own utter freedom beyond Moses's calculation:

> I will be gracious to whom I will be gracious, and will show mercy on whom I will show mercy. (v. 19)

This is a God of grace and mercy, but that graciousness and mercy cannot be programmed, summoned, or predicted. Unlike the gods of Pharaoh, YHWH is not "on call." This remarkable divine utterance permits YHWH to assert grace and mercy, but to do so as a declaration of sovereignty that has a dismissive tone about it.

Because of this wondrous statement of divine freedom, Moses cannot see the divine face—no graven image or any kind of image! The face is too free and too dangerous for Moses to behold.

Finally YHWH makes a small concession to Moses. In a careful choreography Moses is permitted to see the backside (rear end!) of divine glory, but not the face. In the odd paragraph on the tabernacle just above, it is said,

> Thus the Lord used to speak to Moses face to face, as one speaks to a friend. (33:11)

But not in this verse! In this verse, YHWH preserves the hiddenness and inaccessibility of divine freedom. God, unlike the Egyptian gods, is not a function of the state or an apparatus of the economy. This is God unencumbered.

There the matter is left to rest for a moment. The alienation from the golden bull has been acute. Moses's bargaining capacity has been bold and direct, but limited. As a result, Moses must wait. And we must wait with Moses, not knowing. The preacher can attest to this God who is not "on call," not so easily accessible as the reassuring gods of the market, not so accommodating as the gods of commodity.

And then the moment of waiting ends. YHWH engages in a Karl Barth–like self-disclosure:

The Lord, the Lord,
a God merciful and gracious, slow to anger,
and abounding in steadfast love and faithfulness,
keeping steadfast love for the thousandth generation,
    forgiving iniquity and transgression and sin,
yet by no means clearing the guilty,
but visiting the iniquity of the parents on the children
and the children's children,
to the third and fourth generations. (34:6–7)

This remarkable utterance sounds the cadences that persist in covenantal faith. YHWH employs a cluster of terms to characterize fidelity: merciful, gracious, slow to anger, steadfast love, faithfulness, steadfast love (again), forgiving. It is all fidelity. It is all for the maintenance of a relationship. This God is so different from the gods of Egypt in this utterance. That, however, is followed by the big "yet" of unmocked holiness. There is nothing easy or cheap about this covenant. This God knows the vocabulary of alienation—transgression, sin, iniquity—and takes the alienation seriously.

This two-pronged statement voices the cagey, personal quality of this God, not of cheap love, not of angry retaliation, but one who takes covenant with Israel as definitionally hard work. The preacher has a chance to articulate the gravitas of relationship that eschews the easy intimacy of a one-dimensionally friendly god on the one hand, and a relentless punisher on the other hand. In the world of commodity, it is all *quid pro quo,* but here the matter is thick and unresolved.

The response of Moses to this divine self-disclosure is one of humble petition:

> O Lord, I pray, let the Lord go with us. Although this is
> a stiff-necked people, pardon our iniquity and our sin,
> and take us for your inheritance. (v. 9)

Moses does not know. Because this God is not an automaton,
but a free agent. This is a God to whom petition is made: "Par-
don, take us!" But the petitioner does not know and must wait.
And then the utterance of divine resolve, to make covenant, to
perform miracles, to be awesome, to give new futures:

> I hereby make a covenant. Before all your people I will
> perform marvels, such as have not been performed in
> all the earth or in any nation; and all the people among
> whom you live shall see the work of the Lord; for it is an
> awesome thing that I will do with you. (v. 10)

The negotiation has led to covenant restored! But the restoration
of relationship finally depends not on Moses's bargaining, but
on the new enactment of grace and mercy.

It is clearly a mistake to read the initial covenant-making
narrative of chapters 19–24 without attending to the open-
ended process of chapters 32–34. It turns out that the truth
of covenant is not a simple or one-dimensional contract. It is
rather an endless process of breaking and making, of ending
and beginning afresh. The process is one of never arriving, never
absolutizing, never being certain. Because it is an interpersonal
transaction, it is always open, always risky, always holding hard-
gained futures. The preacher, along with the rest of us, lives in
a society that has nearly forgotten the thick hard work of relationship. But it is the truth of Moses's tale. It is the story of
emancipation, abundance, and traded duties. But the draw of
Pharaoh, the draw of certitude and servitude and conformity

and trust in totalism, is enormous. Pharaoh is always coming yet again to power. Pharaoh is always setting new production schedules. Pharaoh is always yet again confiscatory about what we have and need.

Pharaoh must always again be interrupted. And YHWH must always again be reengaged. The preacher invites the congregation into the dramatic storyline that is the story of our life. That storyline, risky as it is, is much too often flattened into something less risky. It is, however, the only alternative to pharaonic rule. The preacher exhibits the costly viability of this dramatic performance that invites relief from the deathliness of a technological system that is thin and simple in endless reductionism.

Covenant Reimagined and Reperformed

Pharaoh, in whatever guise, wants to monopolize the zone of imagination, so that nothing is imaginable outside his realm. The Moses tale is a defiant, hope-filled act of counter-imagination that moves decisively outside the zone controlled and administered by Pharaoh. It imagines a departure from Pharaoh, legitimated by the departure-willing God. It imagines an abundant life of gift-bread, gift-meat, and gift-water not supplied by Pharaoh. It imagines trading the demeaning commands of Pharaoh for the alternative neighborly requirements of YHWH. In its long critical reflection, that tale recognizes that alternative life in covenant with YHWH is not easy to sustain, because the seduction of Pharaoh continues to cause brokenness of covenant. But it also imagines the readiness of YHWH who made covenant to restore covenant when broken. Unlike Pharaoh, this is a God of second chances and many chances after that.

All of this is imagined in Israel at its very foundation. The Moses tale, however, is not a once-imagined narrative. It is a regularly recurring act of imagination. It is, moreover, not simply a textual or cognitive conviction. It is rather a bodily remembrance that requires active dramatic performance in which a counter-life with YHWH is reimagined in contemporary form. Each time performed, this tale evokes and sponsors the formation of Israel yet again, as alternative to Pharaoh as a neighborly option in the world. Thus the tale is one of dramatic reperformance in contemporary mode, a mode that refuses the imposed conditions of Pharaoh. Liturgic time is dramatic time. In that dramatic time Israel, yet again, does *contestation, departure, abundance, alternative obedience,* and finally newness. The process is never completed and never made sure. For that reason the reperformance is essential for the maintenance of the community. It is the wonder of church liturgy that the preacher may lead that reperformance in utterance and gesture, always again a departure to new emancipated obedience. We may identify four such reperformances:

1. It is the continuing and contemporary practice of *Passover in Judaism* that attests the reperformance. Jewish specificity, with its Torah disciplines and its covenantal voice, is always imagining and thinking of the generation of life outside and over against dominant culture.

2. It is often noted that *Second Isaiah* in exile rearticulates the drama of the exodus departure; this time it is departure from the Babylonian empire. There can be no doubt that the powers of Babylonia, notably Nebuchadnezzar, are cast as Pharaoh. Among the texts that show the poet offering a reperformance of the exodus narrative are the following:

✳ the new highway in the wilderness (40:3–5);
✳ the transformation of the wilderness (41:17–20);
✳ YHWH's leadership in a way they know not (42:14–16);
✳ a way in the wilderness (43:14–21);
✳ a new city in the land of promise (49:8–12); and
✳ Israel's departure in joy and peace (55:12–13).[12]

Quite explicit reference to the Exodus is evident, moreover, in 43:16–21; 48:20–21; 51:10; and 52:11–12. Beyond that, chapter 46 mocks the gods of Babylonia and chapter 47 imagines the demise of Babylonia. It is clear that this poetry intends to reinsert YHWH into the imagination of Israel (who had been erased from imagination by the force of empire), and thereby to evoke historical possibilities not otherwise available.

3. By typological imagination it is possible to see *the articulation of Jesus* in the gospel tradition as a reperformance of the exodus. Recent scholarship has seen that Jesus, in gospel tradition, is set in the context of the Roman Empire and offers an alternative to the rule of Rome.[13] Jesus singularly evoked hostility from the local authorities who had signed on to the maintenance and benefits of Roman governance; they perceived immediately that Jesus was a threat to such an imperial governance. His emancipatory work is summarized in his response to the query of John:

> Go and tell John what you have seen and heard: the blind receive their sight, the lame walk, the lepers are cleansed, the deaf hear, the dead are raised, the poor have good news brought to them. (Luke 7:22)

It is exactly that emancipatory work that violated the settled protocols, that evoked hostility and prompted the need for his execution. The contest between the old established governance and the welcome of emancipatory possibility is succinctly put in the narrative of Luke:

> Every day he was teaching in the temple. The chief priests, the scribes, and the leaders of the people kept looking for a way to kill him; but they did not find anything they could do, for all the people were spellbound by what they heard. (Luke 19:47–48)

There can hardly be doubt that the same intent is operative in the figurative language of Paul in his liberation trajectory. Brigitte Kahl has shown that Paul, in his letter to the Galatians, intends to suggest dissent from "the law of the empire" which he sees as a recipe for death.[14] Thus Paul's witness to Jesus, as well as the Gospel narratives themselves, exhibits his authority and force in legitimating life outside of the totalism of Rome. Alan Streett, moreover, has suggested that the early practice of Holy Communion in the church was a subversive imitation of a Greco-Roman practice of symposium.[15] Streett's suggestion gives credence to the notion that this was indeed reperformance, as the early church practiced departure from imperial modes of control.

4. It remains for the preacher to consider contemporary reperformance of the Moses tale. Such a reperformance requires enough social analysis to see that our contemporary dominant ideology of free market claims (coupled with an ideology of US exceptionalism reinforced by the clichés of militarism) is indeed an enslaving enterprise for many. That dominant economy depends on cheap labor and is committed, in systemic ways, to the development of ever greater socioeconomic inequality.

The good news of the gospel entrusted to the preacher is that there are alternative modes of life made possible in a world loved by God and saved through Jesus of Nazareth. Such an alternative, moreover, depends upon departure from the false promises and impossible requirements of the empire of corporate capitalism. That departure surely must take many forms:

* *liturgical*, as the church practices another way, "a more excellent way";
* *emotional*, in order to discover that the forms and expectations generated by the dominant system are imposed and are not givens; and
* *economic*, to order our reliance on commodities in neighborly ways.

None of this is easy, as it was not easy the first time. Of course the preacher will receive resistance from those who have no intent of "departure." And surely the best-intentioned among us—likely including the preacher—will be staggered by such a performance. Moses himself did not want to depart either (Exod 3:13–4:17). The grip that dominant ideology has on our imagination, moreover, means that any modicum of departure is subject to fierce recall, for a return to Pharaoh always sounds attractive.

For all of that, however, it is the preacher's task. Life beyond the reach of Pharaoh is an endless invitation. The summons, "Follow me," is not a call to church membership. It is rather an offer of life outside the totalism, outside the power of death that by way of cheap labor wants to reduce everything and everyone to tradable commodity.

3

Preaching from
the Prophets

A curious thing happens to most of us when we think about texts for "prophetic preaching." Almost invariably we imagine that we are cast in the role of the prophet, most particularly the role of Amos. That is why we have countless paraphrases of the book of Amos. We imagine that we are to give voice to the impatient righteous indignation of Amos or the weeping of Jeremiah, or that we are the one who, alongside Isaiah, said, "Here am I, send me." Here I will suggest that when we face a prophetic text, we face a *text*, not a *role*. Our task is to exposit the text with all of the imagination that we can muster, but we are text interpreters, and not a reiteration of the prophet himself.

Speaking in a Silencing Culture

Every prophet in ancient Israel, from Elijah in the ninth century to Malachi in the fifth century, operated under a regime of steady and intense domination. In the ninth to seventh centuries, from Elijah to Jeremiah and Zephaniah, the regime of dominance was the monarchy, whether of northern Israel in Samaria or the Davidic dynasty of Judah in Jerusalem. After the fall of Jerusalem and its monarchy, the prophets, notably Ezekiel and Second Isaiah, were situated in the Babylonian empire; subsequently Haggai, Zechariah, and Malachi were located in the Persian regime. Of course, each of these regimes—Samaria, Jerusalem, Babylonia, Persia—was distinctive. But they all shared a common commitment to order and control. That order inevitably served its beneficiaries in political and economic ways, regularly sanctioned by a priestly authority. In each case the regime did what it could to maintain itself to perpetuity. Every dominant regime imagines itself to continue without disruption and takes steps to guarantee that continuation.

The *sine qua non* for such continuation is the articulation of a self-justifying ideology that is all-comprehensive and all-explanatory, that allows for no social possibility or economic alternative outside the domain regulated by the regime. Such maintenance, however, is not finally accomplished by overt force or coercion. It is accomplished by the establishment of a monopoly of voice that limits what is said, and that silences voices that are too dissonant from the claims of the regime.

In the Old Testament, it is clear that the royal regime took steps to silence prophetic utterance that was unbearable for the regime and that disrupted the unchallenged and unchallengeable claims of that ideology. Thus Elijah is termed by King Ahab "my enemy" (1 Kgs 21:20); Hosea is dismissed as a madman (Hos 9:7), and Jeremiah is accused of treason (Jer 38:4). These strategies of intimidation aim to discredit the prophet. The most dramatic case of such silencing is that of Amos, who had announced judgment on the royal regime in Samaria. The senior pastor of the biggest church in Samaria, with a clear stake in the well-being of the regime, takes steps to silence Amos:

> O seer, go, flee away to the land of Judah, and earn your bread there, and prophesy there; but never again prophesy at Bethel, for it is the king's sanctuary, and it is a temple of the kingdom. (Amos 7:13)

The silencing, of course, is not just an ancient phenomenon; it continues in our own time. Before the fall of the Berlin Wall, a young East German pastor told me that every sermon he preached was life-or-death, because he knew there was always an observer from the government present in the congregation. It is not so patently so among us. But the notable case of Jeremiah Wright would indicate that the National Security State among us is vigilant indeed to silence voices that are "out of sync" with claims of the dominant ideology. Recent leaks of national surveillance, moreover, put us on notice that we are monitored and, where necessary, silenced in the interest of maintaining the status quo.

Of course, it is not so among us in our congregations. Except that every preacher knows about the silencing that is enforced by the congregation. Every preacher knows about the limit of what can be said, and what must not be said. There are many strategies for silencing in the congregation, most dramatically maneuvers to fire the pastor, but also staying away, cutting pledges, or simply covert hostility. The first line of assault is to say at the door of the church after service, "Better to stay with religion than to tamper with politics and economics." The silencing is real. It is, in its many modes, simply a replay of the old moralistic way of one's mother washing our mouths out with soap after you have learned to say an unacceptable word, even before you knew what it meant. The punishment was not that the soap was so very bad; it was rather the humiliation and the awareness of being vulnerable and finally helpless before the force of silence.

I came to this matter of silencing through a statement of Seamus Heaney, the great Irish poet who died recently. He quoted the French philosopher Gaston Bachelard:

What is the source of our first suffering?
It lies in the fact that we hesitated to speak.[1]

Heaney goes on the say that poetry is the art of breaking the silence. We hesitated to speak because we were not sure. We hesitated to speak because it felt too risky. We hesitated to speak because we had too much to lose. The silence was first broken, in our tradition, when the slaves in Egypt finally "groaned under their slavery and cried out" (Exod 2:23). The slaves did break the silence and cried out. And their cry initiated a new historical possibility. But that report begins, "After a long time." After a long time of silence. After a long time of brutality simply swallowed and humiliation ingested. After perhaps too long a time, the silence is broken. Someone, as you may know, in a cool reflection on the text of Amos, has inserted this remarkable verse in Amos 5:13:

Therefore the prudent will keep silent in such a time;
for it is an evil time.

Maybe this verse is a shrewd, calculating response to the banishment Amos received for his utterance. The term "prudent" can also be rendered as "prosperous" or "circumspect." The circumspect manage to keep their speech inside the safe confines of approved utterance.

The outcome of such prudence, of course, is that much perforce goes unsaid. What goes unsaid is the underside of social reality that the regime does not want uttered. What goes unsaid is the force of human suffering. What goes unsaid is the critique of law that serves only insiders. What goes unsaid is the unbearable violence of the sharp wire and the edge of steel against human flesh. What goes unsaid are those left behind who have no productive value. What goes unsaid is the combination of law, creed, and media that manipulate human sensibility so that we are schooled in not noticing. What goes unsaid is the irreducible reality of divine holiness that cannot be domesticated to serve the status quo. That regime, moreover, wants it left unsaid, because if left unsaid, it is not a social fact with currency. The regime knows well that the saying of the unsaid is the greatest threat to the present stacking of the cards.

Uttering the Unutterable

The prophetic tradition of Israel is a corpus that testifies to this most remarkable reality: prophets *utter the unutterable*. It is astonishing that right in the middle of the Old Testament, sandwiched between the Torah (as ancient defining memory) and the Writings (with their belated proposals for sustaining distinctive identity) is the corpus of the prophets. This corpus attests that canonically the utterance of the unutterable is constitutive for the people of God in the world. It is remarkable that this material made it into the canon to perform two functions: a) to position YHWH as the adversary of God's own people and b) to imagine newness when all the evidence tells otherwise. Here

I will probe what I consider to be four dimensions of this utterance that might illuminate our own work in preaching.

The prophets are *deeply rooted in tradition* that was there before their present contestation.[2] The prophets are not independent operators; they are firmly situated in a tradition that was fully available to them and that apparently still had some currency among their contemporaries whom they addressed. We may identify three foci in that tradition of Torah that are elemental to the prophetic corpus. And if our congregations are not knowledgeable about these traditions, (as most are not), then we have important educational work to do.

At the center of Torah tradition, much more important in subsequent Judaism than in Christian tradition, is the Mosaic narrative of exodus-Sinai. It is impossible to overstate how crucial this narrative is for the prophetic tradition and consequently for prophetic preaching. The exodus narrative is a memory of the way in which the God of emancipation willed the overthrow of Pharaoh's brutal system of production. The narrative provides, to be sure, that the actions are taken by human agents, Moses and Aaron, but clearly it is the initiative of YHWH that is featured; YHWH is allied with the vulnerable in opposition to the regime that is organized as a pyramid club. The narrative begins with the moans and groans of the slaves that finally come to speech. It ends with the triumphant declaration:

The Lord will reign forever and ever. (Exodus 15:18)

It is a story of the way in which the advance of YHWH to the cosmic throne entails the overthrow of enormous power that refused neighborliness. It is clear that the political-economic dimensions of public life are so woven into the narrative that it is impossible to reduce the narrative to mere religion.

As you know, the narrative culminates in the covenant at Sinai. In that ominous narrative confrontation YHWH enunciates ten rules for an alternative society. I judge that the ten rules are counter-rules, counter to the predatory rule of Pharaoh.[3] They deliberately refuse Pharaoh's social organization that is sustained by Egyptian gods (see Exod 12:12). This alternative God comes with an alternative political economy in which there will be, at the outset, no worship of commodities:

> You shall not make for yourself any idol, whether in the form of anything that is in heaven above, or that is on earth beneath, or that is in the water under the earth. (Exod 20:4)

At the conclusion, there will be no acquisitiveness:

> You shall not covet your neighbor's house; you shall not covet your neighbor's wife, or male or female slave, or ox, or donkey, or anything that belongs to your neighbor. (Exod 20:17)

And in between, there will be rest from production and consumption:

> Remember the sabbath day, and keep it holy. Six days you shall labor and do all your work. But the seventh day is a sabbath to the Lord our God; you shall not do any work—you, your son or your daughter, your male or female slave, your livestock, or the alien resident in your towns. (Exod 20:8–10)

The continuous stream of Torah interpretation, in both Priestly and Deuteronomic trajectories, endlessly multiplied regulations in order to bring every aspect of life under the domain of the God of holiness and justice. The intent is to wrest every element of life away from the ideology of Pharaoh.

The second aspect of Torah that operates in prophetic horizon is the narrative corpus concerning the ancestors in Genesis 12–50. Moving beyond source analysis and questions of history of religion, this material is permeated with testimony to the power of God's promise. Claus Westermann and David Clines have provided full inventories of the divine promises of name, land, and especially heir that are carried in this corpus.[4] In every generation of Sarah, Rebekah, and Rachel, the mother is barren until God gives an heir. To be sure, the narrative is cast in patriarchal tones. But the affirmation of faith is that God will do the impossible. Indeed, the divine visitor asks Abraham:

Is anything too wonderful for the Lord? (Gen 18:14)

The question lingers in each generation of the ancestors; the testimony is that nothing is impossible for the God who keeps opening new historical possibilities where none seemed available. It is not a surprise that the exilic prophets who had to give utterance when history had failed Israel appealed exactly to this narrative for evidence that YHWH makes a way out of no way:

Look to the rock from which you were hewn,
and to the quarry form which you were dug.
Look to Abraham your father
and to Sarah who bore you;
for he was but one when I called him,
but I blessed him and made him many. (Isa 51:2–3)

The tradition of Deuteronomy looms large among the prophets, not least Jeremiah. Deuteronomy is a second (*deutero*) version of the Torah in which the Sinai commandments are reimagined and rearticulated in light of the new crisis of Israel in the land when it had forfeited its distinctive identity as YHWH's people. We may identify three aspects of this tradition that are important for the prophets:

First, as Gerhard von Rad had seen, Deuteronomy is endlessly dynamic in its capacity to reimagine Torah in ways that keep the Sinai commands current and contemporary.[5]

Second, Deuteronomy warns Israel that affluence will produce amnesia that will cause the scuttling of covenantal identity:

> When the Lord your God has brought you into the land that he swore to your ancestors, to Abraham, to Isaac, and to Jacob, to give you—a land with fine, large cities that you did not build, houses filled with all sorts of goods that you did not fill, hewn cisterns that you did not hew, vineyards and olive groves that you did not plant—and when you have eaten your fill, take care that you do not forget the Lord, who brought you out of the land of Egypt, out of the house of slavery. (Deut 6:10–12)

Long before Karl Marx, Moses understood that economics goes very far in defining religious possibility. The move into prosperity constitutes a decisive threat to the neighborly tradition of covenant.

But third, Deuteronomy is deeply affirmative of the conviction that the land of Canaan, the land of predatory economics, can be transformed into a viable neighborhood. For that reason, the radical Torah provisions of Deuteronomy line out, in paradigmatic fashion, steps to be taken for an alternative of neighborliness.

All of this, exodus-Sinai, ancestral promises, and the interpretive dynamics of Deuteronomy, was available to and operative for the prophets. The sum of this Torah tradition is that there is a people marked for a distinctive practice in the world, a practice that concerns both *the wonder of being chosen* and *the bite of covenantal requirement.* The tradition managed to keep together the wonder and the bite, knowing that the loss of either would be a deep distortion. It takes no imagination at all to see that monopolistic regimes would always want to silence this tradition:

* The notion of emancipatory alternative is unwelcome to a predatory economy that functions like a pyramid club.
* The open-ended promises of the ancestral tradition are unwelcome in the National Security State, for "security" means to foreclose new possibility.
* The interpretive dynamics of Deuteronomy are unwelcome in a theological orthodoxy that has it all settled.

Thus the emancipatory alternative of exodus-Sinai, the open-ended promises of the ancestral narratives, and the interpretive dynamics of Deuteronomy are utterances of the unutterable. And the prophets are heirs to that memory.

The prophets are propelled by *a deep sense of personal urgency.* We have a text; the text is given to us as a voice. And that voice is infused with a personal agent who speaks with courage and passion. It is clear that not all of the prophetic texts arise from the named person, and we have spent too much time romancing prophetic personalities. Given all of that, the text that moves well beyond the named person is energized and credentialed by that person.

That credentialing is given, most often, in the formula, "Thus saith the Lord." It is a widely shared assumption that this formula does not indicate a claim of "divine dictation." Rather, the formula is a claim of a message from "the divine council," the assemblage of gods (over which YHWH presided) who make decisions about the destiny of the earth. Thus the formula claims "insider access" to the ways of the gods. We may take the formula as merely a literary convention, or we may probe it deeply in psychological ways. However we take it, the voice in the text is sounded by one who has deep insight into the future of the world coupled with acute moral passion. The speaker and all of the derivative speakers that together constitute the prophetic corpus have a sense that the history of Israel—and so the history of the world—is infused with holy intentionality that cannot be outflanked. One result of such holy intentionality is that all other claims, including the ideology of the silencing regime, are rendered penultimate; they will, soon or late, yield to that holy intentionality that characteristically contradicts the intent of the silencing regime. Thus the prophetic voice in the text is thrust, directly and without protection, into the contradiction between holy intentionality and the resolve of silencing regimes. So Amos can say that he had no choice but to speak:

> The lion has roared;
> who will not fear?
> The Lord God has spoken;
> who can but prophesy? (Amos 3:8)

Jeremiah can talk about heartburn if he does not speak:

> If I say, "I will not mention him or speak anymore in
>   his name,"
> then within me there is something like a burning fire

shut up in my bones;
I am weary with holding it in, and I cannot. (Jer 20:9)

That is how such unbearably intense poetry arises, is it not? This is not just artistic speech of one who is cranking out a living by making words. This is one who has been so seized by moral urgency that the utterance cannot be held back. No doubt this is very special poetry; but it is like all such artistry that crowds in and cannot be contained. The regime wants to numb us and narcoticize us so that we do not experience such seizure that takes us beyond ourselves.

I suspect that in "prophetic preaching" we have two ways of engaging this profound moral passion. One way is to be a commentator on the text, to permit the congregation to have access to this ancient seizure of moral passion. The more risky alternative is to recognize that from time to time, we ourselves see so clearly what is going on around us that our dominant ideology does not want us to notice. Such moral passion may arrive at the awareness that the present arrangements cannot be sustained. We may call that "God's judgment." But the more modest recognition is that social relationships skewed by greed, anxiety, and violence are unsustainable. Or such moral passion may arise at the awareness that newness is breaking out among us, and it must be received. We may call that the promise of God being fulfilled. But the newness will be on the ground, however we name it.

In such moments of moral alertness prophetic preaching is plunged into the contradiction between the working of God (by way of judgment and promise) and the dominant ideology that imagines there can be neither divine judgment nor divine promise. The moral passion stays focused on the contradiction; the prophetic personality is not only placed there but is shaped and nurtured at that place of contradiction. "Thus saith the Lord" is simply a shorthand for the capacity to say that all of this poetry of contradiction crowded in on us requires us, vexed by it as we are, to speak it. In the face of the silencing regime, there is, I suppose, always a contest between such silencing and such irresistible moral passion. It will not surprise us that the ancients expressed the same understandable resistance to making such utterance as do we.

One of the grounds for such acute moral passion is that the prophets engaged in *acute social analysis*. They entertained no escape into religious kitsch that avoided all the urgent issues. So Amos can deride excessive religiosity:

Come to Bethel—and transgress;
To Gilgal—and multiply transgression;
bring your sacrifices every morning,
your tithes every three days;
bring a thank offering of leavened bread,
and proclaim freewill offerings, publish them;
for so you love to do, O people of Israel! says the Lord
    God. (Amos 4:4–5)

Or Jeremiah can mock the complacent priestly cadences:

Do not trust in these deceptive words, "This is the temple of the Lord, the temple of the Lord, the temple of the Lord." (Jer 7:4)

So late Isaiah can expose pretend worship:

Yet day after day they seek me
and delight to know my ways,

as if they were a nation that practiced righteousness
and did not forsake the ordinance of their God;
they ask of me righteous judgments,
they delight to draw near to God. (Isa 58:2)

That is, these tradition-grounded speakers, propelled by a personal sense of urgency, refused to limit their thinking and their utterance within the bounds of the dominant ideology of royal-priestly exceptionalism. Preachers can get away with anything as long as the system is not challenged or exposed. But these voices, seized by holiness, sensed that present ideological arrangements were simply strategies without moral significance, so contemporary militarism, and so market ideology. They looked to see beyond establishment assurances that intended to keep real social relationships hidden. And they uttered what could no longer be kept hidden. Social analysis, via Marx or Durkheim, is complex. But a simple form of it is "Follow the money." Who has it? Who gets it? Who administers it? Who lacks it? The prophetic exposé is concerned with systemic matters about which we prefer not to think or speak. So Isaiah can imagine that economic privilege will evaporate:

Instead of perfume there will be a stench;
and instead of a sash, a rope;
and instead of well-set hair, baldness;
and instead of a rich robe, a binding of sackcloth;
instead of beauty, shame. (Isa 3:24)

In that utterance there is no divine agency of punishment or retaliation. It simply will happen as the poet imagines social inversion. Jeremiah's social analysis employs suggestive images and ends with a question that the listeners are expected to ponder:

For scoundrels are found among my people;
they take over the goods of others.
Like fowlers they set as traps;
They catch human beings.
Like a cage full of birds,
their houses are full of treachery;
therefore they have become great and rich,
they have grown fat and sleek.
They know no limits in deeds of wickedness;
they do not judge with justice
the cause of the orphan, to make it prosper,
and they do not defend the rights of the needy.
Shall I not punish them for these things? says the Lord,
and shall I not bring retribution on a nation such as
  this? (Jer 5:26–29)

In this quick utterance Jeremiah cites foreclosure and the exercise of eminent domain. The question intends to haunt. Can one do in orphans and the needy with impunity? The market greed of the power elite said, "Yes we can!" But the question lingers.

Such social analysis may also take a positive tone. In Second Isaiah, the prophet chides Israel in exile for succumbing to the silencing of Babylonia and embracing despair:

Why do you say, O Jacob,
and speak, O Israel,
"My way is hidden from the Lord,
and my right is disregarded by my God"? (Isa 40:27)

But Zion said, "The Lord has forsaken me,
my Lord has forgotten me." (Isa 49:14)

Or Ezekiel can have them say:

> Our bones are dried up, and our hope is lost; we are cut
> off completely. (Ezek 37:11)

The despair arises from the assumption of the givenness of Babylonian reality. The prophets, however, know that imperial givens are penultimate and cannot be sustained. They sound like Bishop Tutu about apartheid:

> Have you not known? Have you not heard?
> The Lord is the everlasting God,
> The Creator of the ends of the earth. . . .
> Even youths will faint and be weary,
> and the young will fall exhausted;
> but those who wait for the Lord shall renew their
>   strength,
> they shall mount up on wings like eagles,
> they shall run and not be weary, they shall walk and
>   not faint. (Isa 40:28–31)

> Can a woman forget her nursing child,
> or show no compassion for the child of her womb?
> Even these may forget,
> yet I will not forget you. (Isa 49:15)

> Thus says the Lord God: I am about to open your graves
> and bring you up from your graves, O my people; and
> I will bring you back to the land of Israel. (Ezek 37:12)

The prophets do not explain; they imagine. But their imagination is not wishful thinking. They know about Cyrus the Persian. They know that Babylonia in its arrogant greed is not sustainable. They know that history will go beyond the control of the regime. They invite their listeners to look deeper and further, to refuse the limits of the regime of silence.

So they utter the unutterable. They seem to know, however, that utterance in linear fashion—like an imperial memo—will not succeed. It will state the contradiction in the terms of the regime, and so be outflanked by imperial reason. They intend, moreover, to reach beneath the reason of the regime to make contact even among those who think they must accept the regime. They do so because they know that even those who have wanted to submit to the reason of the regime know better. They know better because they have been haunted at night when the regime cannot monitor. They know better because they are at night preoccupied with issues that the regime cannot touch, issues of fidelity and betrayal, of hope and despair, of freedom and bondage, all the categories of relatedness that the regime does not want to acknowledge. Prophetic utterance is a bid beneath "sensible explanation" to the ground of holy intentionality that has not yet been domesticated.

And so *they speak poetry*, wild preemptive images and subversive metaphors that cannot be contained in the reasonableness of imperial ideology or the certitude of orthodoxy.

Amos can speak in terms of fleeing a lion and meeting a bear (5:19).

Hosea will speak of "heated ovens" of lust, "hot as ovens" to create social chaos (7:4–6).

Micah will do a piece with the pounding cadence of "cut off":

In that day, says the Lord,
I will cut off your horses from among you
and destroy your chariots;
and I will cut off the cities of your land

and throw down all your strongholds;
and I will cut off sorceries from your hand,
and you shall have no more soothsayers;
and I will cut off your images
and your pillars from among you,
and you shall bow down no more to the work of your
hands. (5:10–13)

Micah says "in that day," but he does not say what day, because this is poetry. It will be the day that terminates national security (horses and chariots) and religious manipulation (sorceries and soothsayers) and every form of self-sufficiency.

Isaiah can imagine the loss of living in luxury like the clothes closet of Imelda Marcos with her many shoes:

In that day the Lord will take away the finery of the anklets, the headbands, and the crescents, the pedants, the bracelets and the scarves, the headdresses, the armlets, the sashes, the perfume boxes, and the amulets; the signet rings and nose rings; the festal robes, the mantles, the cloaks, and the handbags; the garments of gauze, the linen garments, the turbans, and the veils. (3:18–23)

All gone!

Zephaniah can imagine Nineveh in abandonment:

Herds shall lie down in it,
every wild animal;
The desert owl and the screech owl
shall lodge on its capitols;
the owl shall hoot at the window,
the raven croak on the threshold;
for its cedar work will be laid bare. (2:14)

Jeremiah can line out a female camel in heat as an image for Judah's lust for security (2:23).

Poetry is the voice of the unutterable. It refuses conventional explanatory reason. It creeps into the crevices of the barely conscious.

In their study of folk practices of social transformation, John Paul Lederach and Angela Jill Lederach have come to the conclusion, based on their observation of folk culture in trauma, that social transformation is incessantly aural:

> Voice as metaphor suggests other key aspects of health, found primarily in the need to feel close enough to processes that affect daily personal and collective life, such that a sense of meaningful conversation is actually possible. . . . Voice organizes an aural, sound-based metaphor. Sound, interestingly, is multidimensional and multidirectional.[6]

These authors detail the rich range of many voices all together. They quote Jacques Attali:

> For twenty-five centuries, Western knowledge has tried to look upon the world. It has failed to understand that the world is not for the beholding. It is for the hearing. It is not legible, but audible.[7]

They utter the names of the ones to whom social healing must attend:

> We again find here metaphoric themes and challenges to which social healing must attend: *displaced* with the loss of place and the search for home; *speechless* with the loss of voice and the search to speak and name; and *motherless*, without a womb and the search to belong.[8]

They quote from Oumar Farouk Sesay:

> It spurs my pulse to pour
> The passion of my soul
> To make ink for my pen
> When my pen pours poetry
> It crushes the gates of my
> Heart and lets out my
> Pain for the
> Monsters that munch
> The mutton and leave
> The bones for the mongrels
> When my pen pours poetry
> It pours for a social change.[9]

There is of course some distance from the ancient prophets to the evidence of the Lederachs. But the constants are worth noting. There is social suffering. And there is the resilient act of poetry that gives voice to suffering and possibility.

I imagine us living in a culture of silence in which everything is centered in the market ideology in the service of the National Security State. Or perhaps it is the National Security State in the service of market ideology. I imagine that this silencing is powerfully operative when the church meets, for we are mostly products of and adherents to market ideology and the National Security State, and we imbibe that liturgy every day. And then the church meets. It meets in consecrated space, meaning that things are very different here. It gathers around an ancient text. By rote we say, "The Word of the Lord; thanks be to God," or we say, "Praise to you, Lord Christ." We meet with half a notion of different speech. We hope the silence will not be broken, because that is too risky. But we want it broken; we listen for an utterance beyond the regime of death. And then the preacher!

* The preacher is *grounded in the tradition* of wonder and bite to which the congregation half subscribes.
* The preacher has been called into some *holy grounding, partly a personal passion*, partly the order of communal cadences.
* The preacher has read widely and thought deeply about our systemic dislocation and what is happening to *the body politic*.
* The preacher is a *word-manager* and has conjured phrases and images to break the complacent cynicism with which we come to church.

It is the preacher's time. And the silencers are on notice. We have here, in church, what is left unsaid elsewhere. And then the preacher speaks. The unutterable is uttered. And we are plunged into a crisis of new possibility. The preacher dares not say, "Thus saith the Lord." But the gravity of the context says, "Listen up." This is not religious kitsch. This is a never-before-heard summons to obedient freedom.

The Undeceiving Word

Seamus Heaney, it is reported, said in an interview in 1991:

> The poet is on the side of undeceiving the world. It means being vigilant in the public realm. But you can go further still and say that poetry tries to help us to be a truer, purer, wholer being.[10]

His term "undeceive" caught me. The prophets in ancient Israel lived in a deceiving, deceived society. In ancient Jerusalem, the populace was deceived by the falsely reassuring ideology of the royal-priestly establishment. Later, in displacement amid Babylonia and Persia, the Jews were deceived by the promises and prospects of the empire. In both cases, to be deceived meant to be summoned and/or seduced into a make-believe world that was contrary to the realities of human life and contrary to that holy intentionality that permeates all of life. To be undeceived means to be brought face to face with the realities of human life in the world and with the reality of holy intentionality. In good poetry that is not banal, there is, insist the poets, a convergence of *human life and holy intentionality*. It is evident, most particularly in the mantras of Jeremiah, that prophetic poetry has two tasks:

> See, today I have appointed you over nations and over
> kingdoms,
> to pluck up and to pull down,
> to destroy and to overthrow,
> to build and to plant. (1:10)

The first task *of plucking up and tearing down* is to expose the unreality of false claims. The second task of *planting and building* is to conjure (imagine) an alternative realty that is outside the scope of establishment pretense. Prophetic poetry is so difficult and demanding, and so urgent precisely because it contradicts, in the most elemental ways, the assumed, unexamined, uncriticized world fostered by dominant ideology. I will consider in turn these two tasks under the rubric of "undeceiving."

The first task of prophetic poetry (plucking up and tearing down) is to undeceive a world of pretense. The deceptive way in ancient Jerusalem (and Samaria) was confident in being God's chosen people, peculiarly entitled to the gifts of creation and peculiarly protected from the dangerous vagaries of history. This conviction of being an exceptional people was fostered:

* by royal theology that credited David and his family with an unconditional guarantee from God:

> But I will not take my steadfast love from him, as I took it from Saul, whom I put away from before you. Your house and your kingdom shall be made sure forever before me; your throne shall be established forever. (2 Sam 7:15–16)

> Once for all I have sworn by my holiness;
> I will not lie to David.
> His line shall continue forever,
> and his throne endure before me like the sun.
> It shall be established forever like the moon,
> an enduring witness in the skies. (Ps 89:35–37)

* by the temple theology that assumed and assured YHWH's uninterrupted presence in and protection of the Jerusalem temple to perpetuity:

> The Lord has said that he would dwell in thick darkness.
> I have built for you an exalted house,
> a place for you to dwell in forever. (1 Kgs 8:12–13)

* by the "Songs of Zion," the self-congratulatory anthems of the temple of which the best known is Psalm 46:

> God is our refuge and strength,
> a very present help in trouble. . . .
> The nations are in an uproar, the kingdoms
> totter;
> he utters his voice, the earth melts.
> The Lord of hosts is with us;
> the God of Jacob is our refuge. (vv. 1, 6–7)

This convergence of political-liturgic ideology assured Israel, most especially its elites who had access to king and temple, that all will be well. Israel can act with impunity to do whatever it wants; God will take care of you!

Mutatis mutandis, I propose, it is exactly the conviction of exceptionalism that permeates the consciousness and the sub-consciousness of US citizens, a conviction that yields a sense of entitlement, privilege, and moral high ground, that evokes a theory of world management expressed in winsome euphemism. That is why, I suspect, the event of 9/11 has been a durable turning point among us, the unthinkable awareness that we are vulnerable and not safe, that we are at risk, and need to "man up" to protect our advantage.

In ancient Israel the prophets knew better than that all of the time. They knew better because they imagined outside the given system of explanation. They knew that history hosts the wild card of holy intentionality that will not be contained in such a system:

> But will God indeed dwell on the earth? Even the heaven and the highest heaven cannot contain you, much less this house that I have built! (1 Kgs 8:27)

Lord, where is your steadfast love of old,
which in your faithfulness you swore to David?
   (Ps 89:49)

They knew, and so they uttered unutterable poetry. Thus Micah:

Therefore because of you
Zion shall be plowed as field;
Jerusalem shall become a heap of ruins,
and the mountain of the house a wooded height.
   (Mic 3:12)

That remembered ominous utterance of Micah turned out to be a formidable ground of appeal. A century later, it became the proof text in the defense of Jeremiah when he was accused of treason against the state of Judah (Jer 26:18). The prophets imagine, well ahead of events, than a huge sadness is coming to failed Jerusalem. Thus Amos in a dire utterance imagines Israel as a helpless fallen young woman:

Fallen, no more to rise,
is maiden Israel;
forsaken in her land,
with no one to raise her up. (Amos 5:2)

So Jeremiah picks up the theme of a broken helpless woman:

For I heard a cry as of a woman in labor,
anguish as of one bringing forth her first child,
the cry of daughter Zion gasping for breath,
stretching out her hands,
"Woe is me! I am fainting before killers!" (4:31)

This is not, in the poem, the cry of a woman. It is a cry "as of a woman," a vulnerable woman caught in the crossfire of an invading army, a cry like birth pangs, only it is a gasp of death. Only one verse earlier, we are given a sharply contrasting image:

And you, O desolate one,
what do you mean that you dress in crimson,
that you deck yourself with ornaments of gold,
that you enlarge your eyes with paint?
In vain you beautify yourself.
Your lovers despise you;
they seek your life. (4:30)

Israel is mocked as a prostitute waiting for a pick-up by an enemy soldier. The imagery that moves from prostitute to dying woman giving birth is raw and offensive. It intends to be a match for a desperate situation that remains unperceived in deceived Judah. Its offense intends to match the offense of Babylonian boots on the ground in Jerusalem, brought there, says the poet, by holy intentions and failed covenantal responsibility. The imagery means to penetrate the illusion of the city in jeopardy. It is, of course, voiced in patriarchal language that resists transposition. For that reason the poem is a reach toward the most vulnerable in order to voice the most offensive.

His listeners must have wondered, "What could possibly evoke such violence, such rhetorical threat, such wild imagery, such divine anger?" Oh, says the poet, "I'll tell you. Consider yourselves as YHWH's partner whom you have betrayed." And then comes the accusation:

You said, "I will not serve you."

. . . .

How can you say, "I am not defiled,
I have not gone after the Baals"?
. . . .
You said, "It is hopeless,
for I have loved strangers
and after them I will go."
. . . .
Who say to a tree, "You are my father,"
and to a stone, "You have given me birth."
. . . .
[They say to a tree and a stone,]
"Come and save us."
. . . .
My people say, "We are free,
we will come to you no more.
. . . .
You say, "I am innocent;
surely his anger has turned from me." (Jer 2:20–35)

When they heard this poem, they must have responded, "We have said no such thing. We never would." And the poet answers, "Yes—not in so many words, but by act and by policy, you say, you assert autonomy, self-sufficiency, and authority. Your actions speak louder than words." The poet puts words in their mouths. They are, however, words that match act and policy. The intent of the poem is to make visible, audible, and overwhelming the unchallenged social reality of a society that has abandoned its true love on which its destiny depends.

This ideology of chosenness was just assumed. So our ideology of exceptionalism is just assumed. It cannot be criticized because it is a given. We must reperform it at every ball game and every sports event in which the flag of consumerism and its military accompaniment must be celebrated, because the ideology is deep and treasured among us.

Isaiah does it differently with different images. In his famous love song for the vineyard, he treats Israel as YHWH's vineyard that is cherished and worked and watered and weeded with great attentiveness, so that there can be good grapes (5:1–7). But the produce is disappointing:

> He expected justice [*mishpat*]
> But saw bloodshed [*mispach*];
> righteousness [*tsedaqah*] but heard a cry [*tsa'aqah*]. (5:7)

What should be done with such a failed vineyard?

> I will remove its hedge,
> and it shall be devoured;
> I will break down its wall,
> and it will be trampled down.
> I will make it a waste;
> it shall not be pruned or hoed,
> and it shall be overgrown in briers and thorns.
> I will also command the clouds that they rain no rain
>   upon it. (vv. 5–6)

This is a song, a poem, a parable. Nothing is specific; nothing is predicted about Jerusalem. Nothing is said of divine judgment. It is a poem. It lingers in our hearing. It is filled with first-person pronouns that bewilder us and could not be voiced in prose. The verbs cluster around destructiveness—remove, devour, break down, trample, make waste, pruned, hoed, overgrown, no rain. It is death sentence for the vineyard. And when they asked the poet what he meant, he said, "What do you think I meant? Let me recite it again. What do you hear? What do you think you might expect now in the song?" The vineyard is penultimate. It must answer to the vine-dresser. It is expected to produce; that is what vineyards do. When it does not, expect a disappointed vine-keeper. The poem anticipates the cadences of John the Baptist:

> Even now the axe is lying at the root of the trees; every tree therefore that does not bear good fruit is cut down and thrown into the fire. (Luke 3:10)

The poetry insinuates the agency of God into the life of Israel. And when the agency of God is voiced, everyone is called to account, and everyone is on notice. Everything is changed by the poem. This is not hellfire punishment. This is a poem. This is a probe beneath certitudes that cannot be conducted frontally, but only by images that give the listener enough room to breathe. The poetry does not summon to action. It only asks us to notice what had been unvoiced until now and so unnoticed.

Here is a text my class happened to be studying on September 11, 2001.

> For the Lord of hosts has a day against all that is proud
>   and lofty,
> against all that is lifted up and high;
> against all the cedars of Lebanon,
> lofty and lifted up.
> and against all the oaks of Bashan;
> against all the high mountains,
> and against all the lofty hills,
> against every high tower,
> and against every fortified wall;

against all the ships of Tarshish,
and against all the beautiful craft.
The haughtiness of people shall be humbled,
and the pride of everyone shall be brought low;
and the Lord alone will be exalted on that day.
(Isa 2:12–17)

The poem does not need to be "applied" in order to have it be relevant in a contemporary way. On that day in our class, on 9/11, it did not need to be interpreted. Here is a roll call of the citadels of power and privilege: "cedars of Lebanon, oaks of Bashan, high mountains, lofty hills, high towers, fortified walls, beautiful craft . . . humbled, brought low." And the chant that undergirds it all: "against, against, against, against!"

The poem jars. It jars our sensibility as the chosen and entitled. It jars our intimacy with the God who loves and forgives. It jars the way we thought the world was. We are left, in the presence of the poem, to sense what it is like if indeed "God alone will be exalted on that day" (v. 17). This is not poetry that causes trouble or that evokes divine judgment. This is poetry that calls things by their right name. Because there is, in the inescapable traffic of history, a moment of alarm, loss, and dethronement. We know this very well in our gut. The poetry makes it available to us.

Anyone can see that our society is in freefall. We play the blame game and will disagree about it. But the freefall is unmistakable. So Ezekiel:

When anguish comes, they will seek peace,
but there will be none.
Disaster follows upon disaster,
rumor follows rumor;
They shall keep seeking a vision from the prophet;

instruction shall perish from the priest,
and counsel from the elders.
The king shall mourn,
the prince shall be wrapped in despair,
and the hands of the people of the land shall feeble.
According to their way I will deal with them;
according to their own judgments I will judge them.
(Ezek 7:25–27a)

The poem insists that the freefall is not random or meaningless. It is linked to holy intentionality:

And they shall know that I am the Lord. (v. 27b)

It is that holy intentionality that is the peculiar work of prophetic poetry.

Utterances of Hope

It turned out of course that the illusion of chosenness did not prevail. The anticipation of the poets came to historical reality. Jerusalem was plunged into destruction. The leading citizens, the great beneficiaries of chosenness, were exiled and deported to empire, for as long ago as Amos such deportation had been anticipated by the poets:

But they are not grieved over the ruin of Joseph!
Therefore they shall now be the first to go into exile,
and the revelry of the loungers shall pass away.
(Amos 6:6–7)

It is no wonder that the plunge was not only into displacement, but also into despair. The power of Babylonia was immense. The gods of Babylonia seemed beyond challenge, and YHWH had been driven from the field of play. Not only was Israel, in this context, unchosen; but YHWH turned out to be no match for the gods of empire. The Israelites were now deceived into thinking that empire had prevailed. They were deceived into awe before the gods of Babylonia. The poets had tried to break *the illusion of chosenness*; now in the wake of that displacement, suffering, humiliation, and defeat, they had to try to break *the illusion of empire* that produced the despair. Now it is an act of hope that is required. Now it is time to *plant and build*. Now it is time to assert that the future is open beyond failure, because judgment is not YHWH's last word. For that reason, prophetic judgment is not the last poem. The last poem is poetry of possibility that turns on the resolve of YHWH who will break empire and create new heirs, new covenant, new temple, new Jerusalem. All things new!

Remarkably, deep in the abyss of exile in the sixth century, there is an eruption of the poetry of possibility. That poetry must be uttered even though Babylonia thinks it is unutterable. It must be uttered, but not too soon, not before the illusion of easy chosenness has been broken. But then, just then, morning has broken like the first morning. Tears have indeed lingered through the night, but then joy comes in the morning. Already the book of Amos had a conclusion:

> I will restore the fortune of my people Israel,
> and they shall rebuild the ruined cities and inhabit
> them;
> they shall plant vineyards and drink their wine,
> and they shall make gardens and eat their fruit.
> I plant them upon their land,

and they shall never again be plucked up
out of the land I have given them, says the Lord your
 God. (Amos 9:14–15)

Already the book of Hosea had ended:

I will heal their disloyalty;
I will love them freely,
for my anger has turned from them.
I will be like the dew to Israel;
He shall blossom like the lily,
he shall strike root like the forests of Lebanon.
His shoots shall spread out;
his beauty shall be like the olive tree,
and his fragrance like that of Lebanon. (Hos 14:4–6)

Already the book of Habakkuk had ended:

Though the fig tree does not blossom,
and no fruit is on the vines;
though the produce of the olive fails,
and the fields yield no food;
though the flock is cut off from the fold,
and there is no herd in the stall,
yet I will rejoice in the Lord;
I will exult in the God of my salvation.
God, the Lord, is my strength;
he makes my feet like the feet of a deer,
and makes me tread on the heights. (Hab 3:17–19)

Already the book of Zephaniah had ended:

I will deal with all your oppressors at that time.
And I will save the lame,

and the outcast,
and I will change their shame into praise
and renown in all the earth.
At that time I will bring you home
at the time when I gather you;
for I will make you renowned and praised
among all the peoples of the earth,
when I restore your fortunes before your eyes,
says the Lord. (Zeph 3:19–20)

Prophetic preaching is the utterance of hope. It must use concrete imagery, like morning dew and like running deer in order to speak the newness. The undeceiving of tiny, vulnerable Israel is to assure that empire cannot and will not prevail. The matter is more complex among us, for we are the empire. Within empire, however, there is this little company of evangelical poetry that continues to know and say otherwise. There is this gathering of poets right under the nose of empire. This little gathering knows that the posturing of empire, even our own empire, is unsustainable in its military capacity, in its economy of greed, in its politics of exploitation. This little gathering knows, moreover, that the foreclosure of the empire is not the end of the world. It is only the end of a mistaken exceptionalism. Beyond it is a little destiny of shalom that is already now being practiced.

Given all these prophetic endings, Isaiah is the master of undeceiving about despair. He utters the end of empire and imagines it demise:

Come down and sit in the dust,
virgin daughter Babylon!

Sit on the ground without a throne, daughter Chaldea!
For you shall no more be called tender and delicate.
Take the mill stone and grind meal,
remove your veil,
strip off your robe, uncover your legs,
pass through the rivers (Isa 47:1–2).

He allows that YHWH had previously given Israel into the hand
of Babylonia, but the empire had misread its mandate:

I was angry with my people,
I profaned my heritage;
I gave them into your hand;
you showed them no mercy;
on the aged you made your yoke exceedingly heavy.
    (47:6)

The empire is unfamiliar with mercy. Empires that commit no
mercy cannot survive—mercy toward the aging, mercy toward
alien immigrants, mercy toward those left behind, mercy toward
the beloved of YHWH. Isaiah takes on the gods of Babylonia
and imagines that they are homemade commodities with no
substantive power:

Bel bows down, Nebo stoops,
their idols are on beasts and cattle;
these things you carry are loaded
as burdens on weary animals.
They stoop, they bow down together;
They cannot save the burden,
but themselves go into captivity. . . .
Those who lavish gold from the purse,

And weigh out silver in the scales—
they hire a goldsmith, who makes it into a god;
then they fall down and worship!
They lift it to their shoulders, they carry it;
they set it in its place, and it stands there;
it cannot move from its place.
If anyone cries out to it, it does not answer
or save anyone from trouble. (46:1–2, 6–7)

Then, in the midst of the poem and against all the data, the poet
has YHWH assert YHWH's contrast to the imperial gods:

To whom will you liken me and make me equal,
and compare me, as though we were alike? (v. 5)

No one!

Remember the former things of old;
for I am God, and there is no other;
I am God and there is no one like me,
declaring the end from the beginning
and from ancient times things not yet done,
saying, "My purpose shall stand and I will fulfill my
intention,"
calling a bird of prey from the east,
the man for my purpose from a far country.
I have spoken, and I will bring it to pass;
I have planned it, and I will do it. (vv. 9–11)

The bird of prey is Cyrus, the Iranian. Cyrus does not know it,
but he is recruited into divine restoration. The poet sweeps by,
says outrageous things, and intends to break the closed mind
preferred by Babylonia. There is more! There is other! That

"more" and that "other" are propelled by the God who is not contained in the limits of Babylonia.

So they must have wondered: If YHWH is such a big deal, why did all of this happen to us? Why has there been *plucking up and tearing down* before there could be *planting and building*? YHWH responds:

> For a long time, I have held my peace,
> I have kept still and restrained myself (42:14a).

I decided to be dormant. I decided to let matters take their course, and the course of human history is toward the victory of empire. But now:

> Now I will cry out like a woman in labor,
> I will gasp and pant.
> I will lay waste mountain and hills,
> and dry up all their herbage;
> I will turn the rivers into islands,
> and dry up the pools.
> I will lead the blind by a road they do not know,
> by paths they have not known I will guide them.
> I will turn the darkness before them into light,
> The rough places into level ground. (vv. 14b–16)

We have yet another poem that teems with divine agency. Again we have an inventory of active verbs: cry out, gasp, pant; again, "like a woman in labor;" lay waste, dry up, lead the blind, turn the darkness. Cry out against the empire and for Israel. It turns out in this belated poetry that Israel is chosen! Israel has long been *chosen*, then dramatically *unchosen*, and now wondrously *chosen again*. But now chosen to make a new way in the world.

Isaiah finishes with a vision of that new mandate of chosenness. It includes *a practice of justice:*

> Thus says the Lord:
> Maintain justice, and do what is right,
> for soon my salvation will come,
> and my deliverance be revealed (56:1).

It consists in *a welcome* to those whom we would not readily welcome:

> Do not let the foreigner joined to the Lord say,
> "The Lord will surely separate me from his people,"
> And do not let the eunuch say, "I am just a dry
> tree". . . .
> These I will bring to my holy mountain,
> and make them joyful in my house of prayer;
> their burnt offerings and their sacrifices
> will be accepted on my altar,
> for my house shall be called a house of prayer for all
> peoples. (56:3, 7)

It includes *a piety* aimed toward neighbors:

> Is not this the fast that I choose:
> to loose the bonds of injustice,
> to undo the thongs of the yoke,
> to let the oppressed go free,
> and break every yoke?
> Is it not to share your bread with the hungry
> and bring the homeless poor into your house;
> when you see them naked to cover them
> and not to hide yourself from your own kin? (58:6–7)

It moves to *a jubilee of emancipation*:

> The spirit of the Lord God is upon me,
> because the Lord has anointed me;
> he has sent me to bring good news to the oppressed,
> to bind up the broken hearted,
> to proclaim liberty to the captives,
> and release to the prisoners;
> to proclaim the year of the Lord's favor,
> and the day of vengeance of our God;
> to comfort all who mourn. (61:1–2)

New possibility yields new mandate! These are mandates that we have forgotten in the ideology of throne and temple. These are mandates that seem not possible under empire. But now, so the poet lines out,

> Do not remember the former things,
> or consider the things of old.
> I am about to do a new thing;
> now it springs forth—do you not perceive it?
>   (43:18–19)

Behold the newness that the poet will show us. The poet has now uttered and we are, for an instant, undeceived in hope.

Preaching the Imaginative Word

I finish with a note of realism. I am aware that this task can hardly be undertaken in most of our preaching venues. Such poetry would not be tolerated. But that it would not be tolerated is simply a measure of the extent to which we have become enthralled by the claims of empire, ready to accept the explanations of empire. But I want now to reiterate what I said at the outset. What we have in prophetic preaching is not a *role* but a *text*. These texts have dropped out of the repertoire of the church because they do not conform to our deceived condition. But when these texts can be read, heard, shared, and only slightly interpreted, they will do their work of undeceiving. I suspect that most who might hear such a text are deeply deceived, including us. We do not want to be undeceived. But we desperately wait to be undeceived, and we have a profound itch to cut through the lies that pass for reality.

For the preacher to do the work of a poet means to reimagine the meeting place and the meeting time and the meeting of the faithful. It requires that we imagine the church not as a place of certitude that echoes the certainty of exceptionalism and of empire, not as a place of moral admonition and urging, but as a place for imagining that is open, a place for metaphor that is transformative. We do that in order to host breathtaking truth and new possibility. I do not think prophetic preaching needs to be heroic or confrontational. It is rather an invitation; it invites us to attend to this old poetry, mostly forgotten, about which we still say in rote habit, "The word of the Lord; thanks be to God." We do not know how such probing offensive poetry becomes the word of God. But it happens; and it continues to happen! Even among us!

4

Preaching from the Psalms

It is not easy or obvious or usual among us to preach from the Psalms. The Psalms, of course, occupy other important places and functions in the liturgy, but they are treated like forbidden territory by many preachers. In addition to the breathtakingly wide variation of use, sometimes elusive poetic imagery, and a recurring adversarial tone, perhaps the major hindrance to preaching from them is the fact that, with few exceptions, the Psalms are human speech and do not claim to be otherwise. Gerhard von Rad has notably subsumed the Psalms under his rubric of "Response," that, is, talk-back to the initiative of God.[1] For the most part that is true, but where Psalms seem not to be an "answer," they are rather the taking of initiative with God. But whether "response" or not, they are clearly human speech and do not aspire, in the first instance, to rise to the status of "revelation." They are fully from the human side of the great dialogue of faith, and they are properly an articulation of anthropology (the nature of the human) as distinct from theology (the nature

111

of God). As long as preaching is understood, even in an inchoate way, as "top down" revelatory disclosure of God, the Psalms will not do.

But of course, preaching is about the full interaction of God and God's creatures. John Calvin, moreover, has famously judged that one could begin from either side, with God or with humanity, and come to the truth of the gospel.[2] In the Psalms we clearly start from the perspective of human creatures engaged in performance of faith.

From the Human Side

In the Psalms, I propose, we begin from the human side. That reality imposes demands upon the preacher, for it requires some self-disclosure and acute pastoral sensibility in a field where everyone is an expert on their own "human side." What we have in the Psalms, for the most part, is *the articulation of human extremity before God in stylized artistry situated in canonical context.* I propose that four elements in this formulation provide important guidance concerning the Psalms as material for proclamation.

The Psalms probe and voice authentic emotional extremity. If we focus on the two major genres of the Psalter (hymns with an addendum of Songs of Thanksgiving and laments/protests/complaints), we have before us a rich panoply of common human emotional extremity that stretches from awed praise to the desperate neediness of our lives, voiced in recognizable form and familiar cadence. Such recognition and familiarity in form and cadence permit us to channel and contain the rawness and raggedness with which we come to God.

The hymns (and Songs of Thanksgiving) are exuberant articulations of self-abandoning praise and overflowing gratitude, a ready, awed acknowledgment that life in its goodness is generated toward us and not by us. Extremities of thanks voice gratitude for quite specific, identifiable gifts and know the name of the giver of good gifts. Hymns, with less specificity, run toward bottomless awe and wonder concerning the one out beyond us who impinges upon our existence as the one who creates and delivers, and so defies all of our expectations.[3]

Lament, protest, and complaint, by contrast, give voice to the abrasive disjunctions and failures of life that cannot be reduced to guilt. They acknowledge the extremity of deficit that is a reality for very many people that remains very difficult to bring to speech in an honest way.

Psalmic expressions of emotional extremity in our society fall between two ready temptations. On the one hand there is the propensity of a therapeutic culture to "tell all" in a voyeuristic way but without the gravitas or the discipline that might effectively process what is told in transformative ways. On the other hand there is a technological culture that specializes in control, explanation, and solution that eventually leads to denial of the inescapably unsettled quality of human life. In the context of therapeutic culture the performance of the Psalms is an attestation that emotional extremity is not a private property ("all mine"), but is the work of a community grounded in tradition and among neighbors who may be witnesses and respondents to such extremity. The processing of such extremity is a part of the process of making, transforming, and renewing the community and the individual persons as members of that community. In the context of a technological culture, we are made aware of the immense power of emotional extremity that, if not honored in a sustained and serious way, can become a lethal force. Jonathan Haidt, moreover, has made the case that moral decisions among us are for the most part not made on rational grounds, but on emotional grounds.[4] Thus the practice of emotional extremity in the Psalms is an opportunity for honesty that goes along with both taking responsibility for one's extremity and at the same time entrusting that extremity to the community in a way that does not withhold one's self from the neighbor.

The Psalms voice human emotional extremity before God.[5] This God is one from whom no secret can be hid. This means that a voiced psalm is not just a cathartic experience of joy or negation. It is rather a covenantal transaction between two engaged dialogic partners.[6] The matter is important enough that we must be clear that the enterprise of the Psalms is not just an imitation of a tell-all culture. What is voiced here is an act of communion. For that reason the expression of awe or rage is a serious matter to be taken seriously as the one who speaks may withhold nothing from the one addressed. We dare claim, moreover, that the very utterance of praise (thanks) or lament (complaint, protest) before God is an act in which the emotion expressed is handed over to God and is handed back to us in a changed register. It occurs to me that such a transaction is not unlike Eucharistic bread and wine that are "taken, blessed, broken, and given." In the same way hymns of praise addressed to God are taken by God who relishes such praise, are blessed and broken by God's suffering engagement with us, and given back to us as the truth of our life before God. In parallel fashion our voiced laments, protests, and complaints are variously taken by God, blessed by attentiveness, broken by God's self-giving into our troubled life, and given back to us as the truth of our life. Having our emotional extremities received, heard, and honored transforms them and lets them become what they were not, now resources for our faithful reception of life. Emotional extremity submitted to God requires both the relinquishment of having submitted and reception back in changed form that may issue in new power and freedom and resolve.

The emotional extremities voiced before God in the Psalms are expressed in *the artistry of stylized cadence*. The entire program of genre analysis offered by Herman Gunkel is a remarkable recognition that the articulations of extremity—ecstasy and agony—recur in the Psalms as highly stylized, highly disciplined, often repeated patterns.[7] It is for that reason that the Psalms often strike one as repetitious. They are exercises in the way in which this community—which formed, transmitted, and continues to use the Psalms—has cast the very truth of its life. The utilization of the Psalms is a way in which the raw, ragged, and amorphous extremities of our life are framed into a manageable shape that sets limits to the enactment of extremity.[8] The regular usage of the Psalms, accompanied by an intentional pedagogy, can help members of the congregation notice that our community, over many generations, has acquired a stylized way of voicing what is important in our lives. Awareness of that stylized way of speaking can overcome a sense of isolation and abandonment as we stand alongside others who share our particular way of speaking. The preacher can work to induct congregants into a knowing practice or our stylized way of honest speech before God. This stylized way of speaking gives identity over time to the worshipping, singing, praying community.

Gunkel's great insight, moreover, extended to the awareness that patterned speech functions as a vehicle for emotional extremity that regularly arose and occurred in certain kinds of social settings. Those extremities are epitomized by birth and death. Thus the extremities of awe and thanks have to do with the birth of a baby that runs beyond our capacity for speech. This community has tested patterned speech and so knows what to say at the birth of a baby. At the other extreme, death is an extremity that defies our capacity for speech. But the Psalms teach us what to say and how to say amid the wonder of birth and amid the grief of death. Thus Gunkel judged that we can reason backward from utterance to context, so that there is a match between what needs to be said and how it will be said. Inside that patterned framework the particular poet has uncommon freedom in the use of image and metaphor that are kept under the discipline of the form. I believe that liturgical use and especially preaching can be an opportunity to teach and learn the trusted cadences of the community so that "members" of this community of speech learn how we say what must be said about the thickness of our lives.

The individual psalms surely originated in a large variety of contexts under myriad circumstances. Each psalm surely was the utterance (or in a few cases, the writing) of an individual in a specific context. None of these psalms, however, now exists *ad seriatim* on its own. All of them are now in "the book of Psalms," which means that specific psalms have been subsequently resituated in a collection (or originally in a sub-collection). Thus the individual speakers are set alongside companion speakers. And so in our use of the Psalms, we are members of the canonical community that limits and orders the psalms in a larger, settled configuration. Very often it is the "I" who speaks the psalm whom we conventionally identify as David. And very often it is the "we" of the community that speaks. But canonically the "I" or the "we" that speaks is the covenantal community or a member of that community. In subsequent use the entire community participates along with the original "I" or the original "we" in uttering the psalm and voicing our common awe or need.

I suggest that these four features of emotional extremity expressed before God in artistic style in canonical tradition may help the preacher in the proclamatory task. Any particular psalm is an exercise in extremity, but it is before God, it is in a stylized, disciplined way to which attention must be paid, and it is in a framed, shaped tradition. The preacher's task is to authorize and permit members of the congregation to resituate their own extremities of life (and the extremities of the life of the world) in this context. One outcome of such a task well performed is that our emotional life is honored and taken seriously, but it is also resituated before God and among neighbors. This is an exercise that is very different both from much of our therapeutic society that lacks the gravitas for this work and from our technological society that wants to pretend that we are not restless creatures with an undomesticated selfhood of rich energy and imagination.

The entire utilization of the Psalms is a willing, honest performance of self in the midst of community. I anticipate that the performance of the self in the Psalter is much more helpful, authentic, and transformative than much that happens in our therapeutic culture, and much more honest than our technological culture that believes in quick fixes and that fails to reckon with the dialogic unresolve that constitutes human existence.

Performance and Plot

I have deliberately used the term "performance," the honest performance of the self in the midst of the community. That performance is the work of the Psalms and of the preacher of the Psalms. The usage seems appropriate since the Psalms have a musical quality to them. Thus the Psalms may be the score of music (or drama) and preaching is the performance of that score which the congregation can observe or in which the congregation may readily participate. That participation is likely because the subtext of this score is immediately familiar to all parties, the subtext of emotional extremity. With an appeal to the notion of performance, I will consider in turn *plot, character, and context*, the essential ingredients to any artistic performance.

Concerning *plot* I take my lead from Claus Westermann, the most important Psalms scholar of the last generation. In his study of genres following Hermann Gunkel, Westermann has referred to the "Songs of Thanksgiving" as "narrative Psalms."[9] That is, the Songs of Thanksgiving tell a recurring story that includes:

a) a situation of need;
b) a petition to YHWH for help in a circumstance of need;
c) an answer of rescue by YHWH that is acknowledged by the speaker; and
d) a human response to YHWH's deliverance in the form of thanksgiving.

The thanksgiving, as we will see, includes both the narrative retelling of the entire sequence of need/petition/divine response (so the psalm) and a material offering of gratitude, thus a "thank offering."

It is my suggestion that we take this narrative plot as definitional for all the Psalms. And where this notion does not fully work, it will in any case be of exploratory value. Such a plot reflects two convictions, a) that the needy speaker is in the end dependent on YHWH's attentiveness, and b) that YHWH is indeed attentive in transformative ways. I will line out this master plot with two examples from which Westermann has taken his lead.

Psalm 30

The sequences of steps in the experience of this narrator are quite clear:

✳ A sketch of well-being:

> As for me, I said in my prosperity,
> "I shall never be moved."
> By your favor, O Lord,
> you had established me as a strong mountain.
> (vv. 6–7a)

✳ A plunge into trouble:

> You hid your face;
> I was dismayed. (v. 7b)

Then the psalmist tells about his prayer in his dismay:

✳ Supplication:

> To you, O Lord, I cried,
> And to the Lord I made supplication. (v. 8)

✳ Motivational questions:

> What profit is there in my death,
> if I go down to the Pit?
> Will the dust praise you?
> Will it tell of your faithfulness? (v. 9)

✳ Petition:

> Hear, O Lord, and be gracious to me!
> Lord, be my helper. (v. 10)

It is remarkable that in these three verses the name of YHWH is repeated four times, evidence of great intensity. This plot cannot be performed except with reference to YHWH. The plot continues with a resolution of trouble, voiced in direct address to YHWH:

> You have turned my mourning into dancing;
> You have taken off my sackcloth and clothed me with
>   joy. (v. 11)

The Psalm ends with thanks:

> So that my soul may praise you and not be silent.
> O Lord my God, I will give thanks to you forever. (v. 12)

The plot tells the story from *well-being* through *trouble* to *resolution.*

The same plot, given in detail in verses 6–12, is summarized earlier in verses 2–3, each line intensified by the divine name:

✳ Petition:

> O Lord my God, I cried to you for help. (2a)

✳ Divine response reported:

> And you have healed me.
> Lord, you brought up my soul from Sheol
> restored me to life from among those gone
>   down to the Pit. (vv. 2–3)

I propose that this is the primary plot of biblical faith that is already performed in the exodus narrative, and then is reperformed many times by Jesus in his response to needy, vulnerable people. It is, moreover, the primary plot of our daily existence. In telling the story of our lives, we identify this moment of *great need*; we bear witness to *great transformation or great gift*, and the evocation of *great gratitude*. All such retellings of the plot make clear (1) that one cannot always maintain an equilibrium of well-being in one's life, and (2) that help from the outside has mattered decisively. It is easy enough, moreover, to notice that this same plot is the storyline of most TV commercials:

> thus impotence and then the remedy;
> thus loneliness and then the rescue beer;
> thus wrinkles and then the rescue cosmetics.
> thus calamity and then the rescue insurance company.

It is the same plot line of deep need, petition, and responsive rescue. In secular discourse every product can play the role God plays in the evangelical performance of the narrative.

Psalm 116

A second example from Westermann's analysis of narrative songs of thanks is Psalm 116, also a Song of Thanksgiving. The same pattern of speech occurs that we have seen in Psalm 30:

✳ The trouble:

> The snares of death encompassed me;
> the pangs of Sheol laid hold of me;
> I suffered distress and anguish. (v. 3)

✳ The petition:

> Then I called on the name of the Lord:
> "O Lord, I pray, save my life." (v. 4)

✳ The rescue:

> For you have delivered my soul from death,
> my eyes from tears,
> my feet from stumbling. (v. 8)

✳ The response of gratitude:

> What shall I return to the Lord for all his
>   bounty to me?
> I will lift up the cup of salvation and call on the
>   name of the Lord,
> I will pay my vow to the Lord in the presence of
>   all his people.
> Precious in the sight of the Lord is the death of
>   his faithful ones.
> Lord, I am your servant;
> I am your servant, the child of your serving girl.
> You have loosed my bonds.
> I will offer you a thanksgiving sacrifice
> and call on the name of the Lord.
> I will pay my vows to the Lord in the presence
>   of all his people,
> In the courts of the house of the Lord,
> in your midst, O Jerusalem.
> Praise the Lord! (vv. 12–19)

You will see that in my reading I have omitted a few verses, but they are all variations on the basic elements of the plot. The psalm ends with a flood of gratitude that goes on for seven verses. The emotional extremity of "the snares of death" is matched by the emotional extremity of gratitude that reverberates with a ready eagerness for great generosity back to YHWH. I refer to this narrative sequence as the primary evangelical plot because at the center of it is a stunning, inexplicable affirmation that God has acted in transformative ways. It is the preacher's opportunity, I propose, to retell the life of many congregants according to this narrative plot so that the good news of the gospel is at the center of the plot of our life. To be sure, many members who hear the preacher have not experienced that inexplicable transformation; they may linger in the night of trouble or in the much-repeated petition. But all are located in the sequence, either rejoicing in newness or awaiting that pivot point of rescue.

I can think of four ways to generalize about this plot, though you may think of others:

First, this is the plot line of all evangelical preaching since Luther. The "three-point sermon" is three points not simply because it makes for good rhetoric. The sequence is substantive: a) the human predicament, b) the news of rescue, and c) the new life in Christ. The points in sequence tell the elemental truth of our life before God. Obviously, each of these three moments invites to an emotional extremity of despair, awe, or gratitude.

Second, this is the structure of the Heidelberg Catechism, the most important of the Reformation catechisms that was aimed at irenic ecumenical possibility. Its three points of organization are:

* humanity's sin and guilt;
* humanity's redemption and freedom; and
* humanity's gratitude and obedience.

One can see that this structure is exactly parallel in the Thank Songs of Psalms 30 and 116. Except for one matter! In conventional Reformation sermons and in the Heidelberg Catechism, the first theme is "Sin and Guilt," whereas in the Psalms it is *dismay and death*. Israel's great poetry is not ready or willing to reduce the human predicament to sin so that all troubles are rooted in guilt. Instead of that the book of Psalms characteristically entertains the thought that dismay or trouble is not the fault of the speaker, but is due to the work of an adversary, whether an unnamed fellow or an inattentive God.[10]

Third, I have satisfaction in noting that my own typology for the Psalms—as orientation, disorientation, new orientation—follows the same pattern. Indeed, in my book of 1984, *The Message of the Psalms*, I appealed to the three seasons of stability, dismay, and restoration in Psalm 30 as a way to notice the dramatic force of psalms that stands close to lived reality.[11] I am pleased to see that my typology has been broadly accepted among interpreters. In it I have suggested that everyone is located somewhere in this dramatic movement of *orientation, disorientation, and new orientation*. The process continues, moreover, in our lives so that new orientation over time becomes an old orientation that eventually plunges, yet again, into disorientation.

Fourth, the most recent master work on the Psalter by Bernd Janowski is ordered in the same way in two parts:[12]

From Life to Death;
From Death to Life.

He spends a great deal of energy on the abyss at the bottom of death. He appeals to Paul Klee and to an acknowledgment of the deep despair and desire that come to speech in the Psalter.

It will be clear that this grid, in whatever way it is articulated, is indeed a performance of emotional extremity. The plunge into dismay or despair evokes regressive speech of a brutalizing kind that, among other things, issues in a wish for revenge from God. On the other hand, the arrival at new orientation evokes an extravagance of praise and thanks for an unbelievable, new permit to live in freedom and well-being. The preacher, by appeal to the Psalms, has a chance to recast daily life in the midst of the defining narrative. Such a recasting is an antidote a) to an easy bourgeois complacency that imagines that a good status quo will last forever, b) to despair that there can be no rescue, so deep is the trouble, and c) to stifled rage and anger that are brought to speech as an act of vigorous faith that submits such urgency to the reality of God.

Now it will be clear that only a few psalms tell this entire narrative. It is my thought that without too much coercion but with some imagination, that any particular psalm can be seen as a voice for some element of the plot at some way station along the path of life. Thus for example, one could take Psalm 37 (a wisdom psalm), or Psalm 15 (an entrance liturgy), or Psalm 119 (a Torah psalm), as expression of well-being in orientation that acknowledges the good fidelity of the creator God. There are indeed wondrous moments of equilibrium in our lives that need to be cherished and acknowledged as gifts from God.

In the second place, many psalms of lament and complaint reflect dismay, disaster, or even death. It is in these psalms that one hears voiced shrill hate and resentment and proposals to God about appropriate vengeance. These "not nice" psalms may offend those who live in a safe, stable, prosperous, properly ordered life. The Psalms know, moreover, via Psalm 88, that there are no automatic deliverances from the abyss; one must wait in hope and in rage, but never doubting that newness is possible.

In the third place, arrival at newness evokes elation and jubilation. In addition to Songs of Thanksgiving, the entire inventory of doxology belongs to this moment. One did not expect to be healed. One cannot explain how that newness was enacted. But the rhetoric soars at the reality. There are, as Westermann has seen, psalms that identify particular acts of rescue. And there are psalms that move past such particularities to a generalized praise that speaks of God's unutterable fidelity.[13] Specifically, the Enthronement Hymns that mark God's return to governance are a celebration that the center holds and that the world works.

I propose that in taking up any particular psalm, one ask, "How does this psalm bear witness to what part of the master narrative of the Psalter?" Such a question permits us to recognize that this moment in the plot was important enough that there was a pause long enough to offer a new poem. It also reminds us that this moment in the narrative is not the whole of the narrative, and other members of the community may just now be elsewhere in that narrative.

If one is to appeal to the master narrative, then it is imperative to ask, "How does this instance serve the larger plot?" That question about a particular psalm has its counterpart in the pastoral practice wherein one may ask of any particular moment:

How does this moment in our life relate to a master narrative that our life performs? How does the larger plot make sense out of this psalm?

How does the master plot of your life illumine this moment in your life?

> How does a new baby or a new job or a new diagnosis fit the plot?
>
> Or did you know this was the plot of your life?
>
> Or do you need to edit the plot of your life to take this moment into account?
>
> Or do you need to revise your notion of the Psalter to take this Psalm seriously?

We often cite psalms *ad seriatim* (one by one) without regard to the larger plot that works through them. We thereby encourage folk to take any moment of their lives *ad seriatim*. It is, however, the task of the preacher to insist on the larger plot, and to exhibit the ways in which God occupies every moment of the plot, sometimes for good, sometimes for ill. Everyone benefits from having the narrative plot of our lives reperformed, especially when it is done with imaginative sensibility to a great moment of emotional extremity in the course of that larger narrative plot. The reperformance of the whole has creditability when the larger narrative and the immediate moment are well linked together. It is like linking a particular psalm to the larger plot of the corpus. The preacher, with the spirit, has a singular chance to do just that!

Performance and Character

My second probe, after plot, is to ask about *character*: Who is speaking? Who is performing the plot? To whom is this psalm assigned? Interpretation will usefully press toward specificity. At the outset we must say that the Psalms, with few exceptions, are anonymous. They have simply welled up in the long stream of tradition. Some few are "learned" psalms, carefully created by temple professionals. But most of them are simply acts whereby the community made the case, "This is how we talk." In each case there was a "first talker." In Christian tradition there is a long practice of claiming that the righteous sufferer who speaks in the Psalter is none other than Christ. That practice was compellingly undertaken by Augustine and then utilized by Dietrich Bonhoeffer. Jason Bayasee has most recently urged such a reading, but he has done so with very little actual textual discussion.[14]

Somewhere between the recognition that the character who speaks is an anonymous member of the community and the church's claim that it is Christ who speaks, the more popular claim is that these are the psalms of David; it is David who speaks them. That would help us, because the tradition has remembered a great deal about the character of David. This claim is helped along by the fact that nine psalms have superscriptions that explicitly link the psalms to episodes in the life of David (Pss 3, 34, 51, 52, 54, 57, 59, 60, 63). The best known of these is Psalm 51, the great confession of sin that the church utilizes on Ash Wednesday. The superscription (not even noticed in the Book of Common Prayer) is:

> *When the prophet Nathan came to him, after he had gone in to Bathsheba.*

The superscription makes a link to the narrative of 2 Samuel 11–12. Perhaps it is a bit puckish, as the verb translated "gone in," that is, into the bedroom, can also be translated, "entered," that is, "entered Bathsheba." The other psalms have like superscriptions that link to specific narratives concerning the life of David. Some of them fit well, some are quite ill-suited to the narrative.

In any case, critical scholarship has consistently judged that while these superscriptions are of course canonical—they are in the text!—they are surely secondary, belated hints in the tradition about how the psalms might be read. Thus:

* Psalm 3—"when he fled from his son Absalom."
* Psalm 34—"when he feigned madness before Abimelech so that he drove him out and he went his way."
* Psalm 52—"when Doeg the Edomite came to Saul and said to him, "David has come to the house of Abimelech."

Most of these connections do not work so well; but in any case they feature a specific character displacing the anonymous voice of the tradition. Thus Brevard Childs, in his classic article, can conclude:

> The Psalm titles do not appear to reflect independent historical tradition but are the result of an exegetical activity which derived its material from within the text itself.[15]

Childs accents the variety and freedom of such interpretive efforts that are reflected in the superscriptions:

> Above all, one senses the variety within the canonical process. Although the Psalms were often greatly refashioned for use by the later community, no one doctrinaire theology was allowed to dominate. . . . The most characteristic feature of the canonical shaping of the Psalter is the variety of different hermeneutical moves which were incorporated within the final form of the collection.[16]

Given that belated interpretive move that reassigns psalms to a new character, David (or even a later reassignment to Christ), here is my thought about the work of the preacher: the Psalms are best interpreted with a specificity of character so that the speech is the actual speech of a known agent. That specificity, however, is wondrously transportable. We commit that move of transport all of the time without great reflection. We transport the specificity of David to the specificity of our own lives, because we find the plot of David's life to be compellingly the plot of our own lives. Thus in Psalm 23, listed as "a Psalm of David," when we read or recite it, it is our "valley of the shadow of death," it is "a table set before us in the presence of our adversaries," it is our "cup that runneth over," it is our resolve to "dwell in the house of the Lord forever." For the most part we do not linger over David or over Christ; we draw the psalm close to our own life and so take the plot as our plot.

It is this transportable specificity that opens up the question of character: Who speaks? Brevard Childs and many scholars have judged that the superscriptions are belated interpretive maneuvers. I propose that the preacher continue the practice of belated interpretive maneuver by proposing, either explicitly or tacitly, new superscriptions that relocate the psalm and its part of the plot in contemporary life. The articulation of new superscriptions, as guides to reading, may serve to trigger our imagination and so cause us to reread the psalm.

I came to this awareness of interpretive possibility when, a long time ago, we were in class reading Psalm 109, a psalm that is filled with vengeance. The speaker, in a fictive courtroom, suggests to the judge the appropriate punishment that should be given to the guilty party. It is rather like the contemporary practice of inviting survivors of a crime or the family of the victim of a crime to speak in court. The speaker says with urgency to the judge:

> When he is tried, let him be found guilty;
> let his prayer be counted as sin.
> May his days be few;
> may another seize his position.
> May his children be orphans, and his wife a widow.
> May his children wander about and beg;
> may they be driven out of the ruins they inhabit.
> May the creditor seize all that he has;
> may strangers plunder the fruits of his toil.
> May there be no one to do him a kindness,
> nor anyone to pity his orphaned children.
> May his posterity be cut off;
> May his name be blotted out in the second generation.
> May the iniquity of his father be remembered before
>   the Lord,
> and do not let the sin of his mother be blotted out.
> Let them be before the Lord continually,
> And may his memory be cut off from the earth.
>   (vv. 7–15)

This torrent of vengeance is so thick and relentless that we cannot bear to read it out loud. As we read the psalm, I asked the class, as I always did, "Who is speaking? Whose psalm is this?"

Without missing a beat, Linda, a Disciples of Christ pastor, said, "This is the speech of a woman who has been raped." And that was a long time ago, before we got much public testimony from women who had been raped. Well, of course, because women have experienced rage and humiliation about rape for a long time, long before it became permissible to go to court. Now the rage of the psalm becomes not only credible but permissible and persuasive; we connect it to a specific context with which we can empathize. We now read the Psalm more knowingly. This is not:

* the voice of an anonymous person in the tradition without context;
* the voice of David, even though the superscription we have says "Of David"; or
* the voice of Christ.

This is the voice of Linda, or of a host of other women who understand that the practice of sisterly solidarity is elemental to the human enterprise. So she can pray:

May there be no one to show him kindness (*hesed*) . . . no one! (v. 12)

And the reason is,

He did not remember to show *hesed*,
but pursued the poor and needy,
and the brokenhearted to their death. (v. 16)

Finally, the speaker turns away from rage to hope as she prays,

Save me according to your steadfast love [*hesed*]. (v. 26)

It may be that the preacher will not readily connect the psalm to Linda or any of myriad other enraged women who sit in the congregation. Maybe the preacher will make this link tacitly. But the linkage will help us to see that such a cry for vengeance is not unthinkable or unutterable. It belongs to honest social discourse. It belongs to the plot as the wounded, aggrieved, and exploited state their case in a way that permits them to move to a good resolution in the morning after a long night of lingering tears.

It may be that the preacher—and the congregation—will sense this psalm to be remote from their experience because many church people live in safety where such things never happen or are never acknowledged to have happened. In that context, the psalm is an invitation to get our minds off ourselves in order to engage in other venues where violence, rage, and dehumanization are endemic—some by terrorists, some by our own military, and some in our own tribes where our economics creates venues for self-hatred and propels to violent conduct.

This psalm moves the plot along. Linda and her ilk do not stay forever in a mood of vengeance; by verse 21 when the rage has been fully voiced, the plot on the lips of such a woman turns:

But you, O Lord, my Lord,

The rage turns to petition:

Act on my behalf for your name's sake;
because your steadfast love is good, deliver me. (v. 21)

That is, I do not ask you to act for me. Rather act for your reputation. You want to be known as redeemer and savior; then act! Do not linger in safe places, but go to where rescue is urgent. Go to my life! Go our life! Go to our violence and terror. There show your *hesed!* Such a moment in the larger plot requires a character who will run the risk of honesty and exposure. The psalm invites us to stand alongside this speaker whom we can well imagine. Because the character who speaks in this psalm is not remote from us.

Here are six other proposed superscriptions that go along with "For Linda as she responds to rape." You might think of others:

Psalm 65:9–13 superscription: "A congregation in Texas when the severe drought had been broken."

You visit the earth and water it,
you greatly enrich it;
The river of God is full of water;
you provide the people with grain,
for you have prepared it.
You water its furrow abundantly,
settling its ridges,
softening it with showers,
and blessing its growth.
You crown the year with your bounty;
your wagon tracks overflow with richness.
The pastures of the wilderness overflow,
The hills gird themselves with joy,
The meadows clothe themselves with flocks,
The valleys deck themselves with grain.
They shout and sing together for joy. (vv. 9–13)

Psalm 85:10–11 superscription: "When Peter and Andrew found a peaceable settlement of their father's estate" or "When Israel and the Palestinians finally made the agreement that everyone knew had to be made."

Steadfast love and faithfulness will meet;
righteousness and peace will kiss each other.
Faithfulness will spring up from the ground,
and righteousness will look down from the sky.
        (vv. 10–11)

Psalm 145:15–16 superscription: "The dedication of a new food co-op."

The eyes of all look to you,
And you give them their food in due season.
You open your hand,
satisfying the desire of every living thing. (vv. 15–16)

Psalm 44:9–14 superscription: "A Psalm of Rage after 9/11" or "A Psalm of Rage after another atrocity in Jenin."

Yet you have rejected us and abased us,
and have not gone out with our armies.
You made us turn back from the foe,
and our enemies have gotten spoil.
You have made us like sheep for slaughter,
and have scattered us among the nations.
You have sold your people for a trifle,
demanding no high price for them.
You have made us the taunt of our neighbors,
The derision and scorn of those around us.
You have made us a byword among the nations,
A laughing stock among the peoples. . . .
All this has come upon us,
yet we have not forgotten you,
or been false to your covenant. (44:9–14, 17)

Psalm 88 superscription: "A psalm of a mother in Baghdad whose son has had his legs bombed off."

For my soul is full of troubles,
and my life draws near to Sheol.
I am counted among those who go down to the Pit;

I am like those who have no help,
like those forsaken among the dead,
like the slain that lie in the grave,
like those whom you remember no more,
for they are cut off from your hand.
You have put me in the depths of the Pit,
in the regions dark and deep.
Your wrath lies heavy upon me,
And you overwhelm me with all your waves. (vv. 3–7)

Psalm 150:3–6 superscription: "The day Sarah received her law degree."

Praise him with trumpet sound;
Praise him with lute and harp!
Praise him with tambourine and dance;
praise him with strings and pipe!
Praise him with clanging cymbals!
Praise him with loud clashing cymbals!
Let everything that breathes praise the Lord!
Praise the Lord! (vv. 3–6)

The preacher's task is to transport specificity from there to here, from then to now. The moment of utterance may be for ourselves as we usually want it to be. It may be for a neighbor or it may be for a stranger who requires our intercession and our solidarity. Such utterance may be kept close at hand. Or it may evoke great imagination in order to move our solidarity and our empathy beyond the usual confines of our own tribe.

Performance and Context

Given the *plot* that moves from need to gratitude, from absence to presence, and given the *characters* who occupy our world of emotional extremity, we may consider, thirdly, how attention to plot and character is situated in *particular context*.

We know very little about the specific contexts of the psalms in the Old Testament. We know about the context of Psalm 137 in the strangeness of Babylonia that evokes cries for vengeance. But even Psalm 137 is transportable. Thus Ernesto Cardenal, in Central America, can say it this way:

> By the rivers of Babylon
> There we sat down and wept
> And there we wept
> As we remembered Zion.
> Looking at the skyscrapers of Babylon . . .
> A Babel armed with Bombs. Devastating!
> Blessed are those who take your children
> —the creatures of your laboratories—
> and smash them against the rocks![17]

The linkage that Cardenal makes from the south toward the Colossus of the North invites us to notice the context in which we may utter these Psalms.

Our context is a *culture of denial* that wants to acknowledge nothing of the self-destructive commitments of our society. We continue to imagine privatization as a cure-all—private schools, ghettoed gated houses, private medical care, all in a readiness to sacrifice the common good and expect that we will be given safe passage by not noticing.

A culture of denial in turn creates an illusory *sense of self-sufficiency*. If we are rich and powerful and smart enough, we can secure our own future. We can fend off again and again requirements of the public infrastructure; we can outflank a despoiled environment; because there is always one more quick fix that will see us through yet again.

Ours is a *culture of despair* in which we silently accept the reality that there are no new gifts to be given, and there really are no solutions to the crises we face. For that reason it is best to live complacently and compliantly within the dominant system of military consumerism, not think outside the box, not rock the boat of injustice. We may hope to get through the course of our lives without any sacrifice for the sake of our grandchildren who will receive from us a closed, failed world.

That *culture of denial, self-sufficiency, and despair* is, I propose, the cultural context in which we read the Psalms. That culture, moreover, is reinforced by a church that settles for "orthodoxy" or for "spirituality" or for a kind of theological kitsch of good feeling in which the gospel must be carefully misread in our preferred way. So the church colludes!

When we notice in discerning ways the package of denial, self-sufficiency, and despair, we become acutely aware that the Psalms are indeed countercultural concerning our culture:

* The laments *refuse denial* and tell the truth about God and about neighbor and about ourselves.
* The hymns *refuse self-sufficiency* and endlessly push the reference point of life out beyond us to the Thou of resolute lifegiving intention.
* The combination of lament and hymn that constitutes the plot of the Psalms *refuses despair*.

Lament and hymn together insist on engagement and risk of the unsettlement of our life that comes to us through emotional extremity. The lament refuses denial and expresses rage, anger, sadness, and ends in hope. The hymn acknowledges generative reality beyond us and permits yielding of all of our sufficiency to the God who has created us. The interplay of lament and hymn requires that we be dialogic creatures who refuse every settlement of certitude and control. We know, in the Psalms, that life is not given in the safe middle ground of management. In anticipation of what Christians call "the mystery of faith," the Psalms know that life is given:

* in Friday anguish of lament, protest, and complaint;
* in Sunday ecstasy of praise and thanks;
* and then we say, "Christ will come again."

In that affirmation we declare that God keeps the world open beyond all of our denial, self-sufficiency, and despair. It is a ludicrous thing to say! But they said it long ago in the great Enthronement Psalms:

> Say among the nations, "The Lord is king!
> The world is firmly established;
> It shall never be moved.
> He will judge the peoples with equity."
> Let the heavens be glad, and let the earth rejoice;
> Let the sea roar, and all that fills it;
> Let the field exult, and everything in it.
> Then shall all the trees of the forest sing for joy
> before the Lord, for he is coming,
> for he is coming to judge the earth.
> He will judge the world with righteousness,
> and the peoples with his truth. (Ps 96:10–13)

Let the sea roar, and all that fills it;
the world and those who live in it.
Let the floods clap their hands;
let the hills sing together for joy
at the presence of the Lord, for he is coming
to judge the earth.
He will judge the world with righteousness,
and the peoples with equity. (Ps 98:7–9)

Coming soon! Not yet finished! Open-ended! Coming with equity, justice, and righteousness![18]

That coming:

* *overrides denial* with the full force of presence;
* *vetoes self-sufficiency* with mystery beyond us;
* dismisses technological fixes and *refuses despair.*

This anthem must be the most succinct articulation of the gospel:

Say among the nations,
YHWH is king,
YHWH has just become king,
YHWH is becoming king.
YHWH will win out . . . thine is the kingdom, the
power and the glory!

The Psalms thus are a great act of defiance against the order of the day! The Psalms in fact reconstruct and reformulate our context. The Psalms contradict what we thought was our context of denial, self-sufficiency, and despair. The ground for reconstruction and reformulation is the character of YHWH, that other character in the plot of the book of Psalms, the one addressed, the one summoned, the one petitioned, the one reprimanded. What a wonder that our lives and the life of the world are marked, always, by a crisis of fidelity—not a crisis of money or power or control, but of fidelity that is crucial but never settled. That is why we meet here, in these poems, emotional extremity. Our emotional extremities are taken up in the crisis of fidelity—our infidelity, the infidelity of neighbors, and even the infidelity of God. And then we are overwhelmed by surges of fidelity that we did not expect.

It turns out that the plot of the book of Psalms is at every step God-occupied. It turns out that all of the interesting characters in the book of Psalms—David, Linda, Texas, Andrew and Peter, Sarah—are all performing their lives in the presence of God or in the absence of God.

But the God who occupies the book of Psalms, alongside all of those notable characters, is not the one-dimensional God of sweet church offering or the judging God of ferocious orthodoxy. This is the God who operates with a full range of emotional extremity,

* in defiance of all human authority;
* in defiance of popular spirituality;
* in defiance of flat-coded evangelicals;
* in defiance of self-confident progressives;
* in defiance of neo-atheists who will allow for no wildness beyond their scientism; and
* in defiance of settled explanatory reason.

This is a God who dwells in the spectacular awe of praise, who is enthroned on the praises of Israel, who requires a myriad of images and metaphors in order to be spoken rightly, because any one by itself is idolatrous. This is a God who enacts the daring abyss of absence wherein we wonder why we have been abandoned. This is not "the God of the gaps" who becomes our explanatory rule for our inexplicable mysteries, for this God does not traffic in explanations.

Thus I propose that every preacher—in some mode—refers life back to God and imagines an emancipated partnership with God that refuses every idolatrous safety and very convenient settlement. Every psalm pushes to some extremity; when we go there we find God occupying that extremity before us, for this God knows about agony and ecstasy, about presence and absence. The Psalter is all human speech. It turns out, however, that this human speech is made possible—and serious and urgent—because of the one to whom it is addressed. Thus we find a double work—as Paul Ricoeur has seen—of *discovering* what is there and then *inventing* what is to be there. The both/and of *discovery and invention* in the artistry of the Psalms constitutes an act of sketching out a world not given anywhere else.

The preaching task is to re-script our imagination with freedom and courage and candor. Our imagination is mostly scripted in quite conventional ways, according to the liturgies of the media or patriotism or our special tribe. But now we are able to see:

* that this is our plot and we are performing it, always tears that linger through the night and joy that comes in the morning.
* that we are and our neighbors are key characters in the performance of this alternative plot, and our performance matters mightily to the future of the world.
* that the plot and our performance of it draw us into the crisis of fidelity with the God who occupies the plot and

bids our engagement with the lament of tears through the night and the hymn of joy in the morning.

The outcome of the plot is praise. So the Psalter ends:

Praise the Lord!
Praise God in his sanctuary;
Praise him in his mighty firmament!
Praise him for his mighty deeds;
praise him according to his surpassing greatness! . . .
Let everything that breathes praise the Lord!
Praise the Lord! (Ps 150:1–2, 6)

After this I looked, and there was a great multitude that no one could count, from every nation, from all tribes and peoples and languages, standing before the throne and before the Lamb, robed in white, with palm branches in their hands. They cried out in a loud voice saying,

"Salvation belongs to our God who is seated on the throne, and to the Lamb!"

And all the angels stood around the throne and around the elders and the four living creatures, and they fell on their faces before the throne and worshiped God, singing,

"Amen! Blessing and glory and wisdom
And thanksgiving and honor and power and might
be to our God forever and ever! Amen." (Rev 7:9–12)

Then the seventh angel blew his trumpet, and there were loud voices in heaven, saying,

"The kingdom of the world has become the kingdom of our Lord

And of his Messiah,
And he will reign forever and ever."

Then the twenty-four elders who sit on their thrones before God fell on their faces and worshiped God, singing,
"We give you thanks, Lord God all mighty,
Who are and who were,
for you have taken your great power and began to reign.
The nations raged,
but your wrath has come,
and the time for judging the dead,
for rewarding your servants, the prophets,
and saints and all who fear your name,
both small and great, and for destroying those who destroy the earth."

Then God's temple in heaven was opened, and the ark of his covenant was seen in his temple; and there were flashes of lightning, rumbles, peals of thunder, and an earthquake, and heavy hail. (Rev 11:15–19)

We shall finish, it is promised, with Charles Wesley, "Lost in wonder, love, and praise." But the process that will end in praise is risky. It is a move through pain, brutality, and absence. But this is our life in the crisis of fidelity:

* This is the life of a church leader in my congregation who loses his home via unemployment.
* This is the life of a woman in my congregation who lost her daughter and has found new life in presiding over a shelter for homeless persons.

* This is the life of a guy in my congregation who every week sends a sermon summary to his grandchildren; he still thinks that it is all working!
* This is the life of an old guy in our congregation who is alienated from his older son and lives in hope.
* This is the life of grandparents in our congregation who have watched brain surgery for their three-week-old granddaughter, and she is well!
* This is the life of a high school graduate in our congregation who was into substance abuse, but who, after a year in college, is on a trajectory to well-being and freedom, and his parents in amazement say, "Is this real?"

It is no wonder that we linger in the company of those who perform this plot and engage the crisis of fidelity, refusing denial, self-sufficiency, and despair. It is no wonder that we say,

I was glad when they said unto me,
Let us go to the house of the Lord.
I was glad when they said to me, "Let's go to church."

Let us go to the place where they keep the poetry of death and life alive. Let us be in the company of those who know about the emotional extremity of lingering tears of rage that must be addressed to the throne and about the soaring hallelujahs of surprising awe. Let us go in companionship with those who know how to speak the truth of the depth and the wonder of the height, and who are not afraid. The book of Psalms arose from a context, but this is also a context-generating book. The book arose in human utterance. But that human utterance is evoked by the one addressed who awaits our speech.

All of this is brought to speech!

All of this is brought to speech in stylized ways, stylized so that it is transportable.

All of this is brought to speech and addressed to the God of fidelity and infidelity.

All of this is brought to speech in the company of ancient saints and present singers.

All this is handed back to us in two-way communication, now blessed and broken.

All this is the script of emancipation and transformation.

All of this . . . and it is on the lips of the preacher. The preacher is the one who understands the plot that is reperformed. The preacher knows the ways in which the characters are transformed by the performance of the plot. The preacher is the one who steps into the context of the crisis of fidelity. The preacher is a child of this poetry and its inescapable persistent advocate.

5

Preaching from the Wisdom Traditions

The wisdom traditions of the Old Testament have been something of a stepchild in recent Old Testament theological study, because theological interpretation has been focused for a long while on the normative credal texts that feature the activity of God. The wisdom traditions (that in the conventional Protestant canon include Proverbs, Job, and Ecclesiastes) largely eschew the covenantal categories of the narrative traditions so they do not yield historical material. A while ago Walther Zimmerli offered the helpful dictum, "Wisdom theology is creation theology." The focal intent of the wisdom tradition is on creation. It is not doubted in the tradition that creation is the sustained generative gift of the creator; but the wisdom tradition does not, for the most part, expend great energy on theological imagination concerning the creator, though much may be inferred. Rather the focus is on creation as distinct from the historical, covenantal memory of Israel.

The upshot of this is that the wisdom traditions of the Old Testament have a great deal in common with like traditions elsewhere in the ancient Near East with much less interest in the peculiarity of Israel or Israel's faith. The material consists in an articulation of a "common theology" that for the most part does not insist on the specialness or peculiarity of Israel, and for the most part does not consider that God would actively intervene in the world, that is, "act in history" as God does so readily in the narrative traditions of Israel.

A positive outcome of this distinctive feature of the wisdom materials, in contrast to other materials in the Old Testament, is that these materials make easier and more compelling contact with our contemporaries who think in "secular" ways about the world and who are not interested in or persuaded by frontally "theological" or "confessional" rhetoric. Those "secular" folk who trust in the scientific "explanability" of the world in reasonable categories without excessive appeal to any "supernatural" considerations, in our context, constitute what Schleiermacher (the great nineteenth-century theologian) termed "the cultured despisers of religion." These are folk who may conclude that religious claims are nothing more than outmoded forms of superstition, but who nonetheless are interested in and preoccupied with "questions of meaning." Such "questions of meaning" (with the mantra of "spiritual but not religious") may probe the irreducible mystery of the world: What is the world like? What is my place in that world? What is the future of the world? Such "wonderments" may indeed invite "wonder" because the world, for all to see, is grand, complex, and defiant of our explanatory categories. Soon or late such "questions of meaning" will come to the "problem of evil" that defies all of our best thinking. Thus the wisdom tradition belongs in the orbit of our deepest, most central, most honest wonderment about the world and our life in it. The madness and glory of wisdom teaching is that it remains restless and open-ended. It is as though the creator God continues to outflank our rationality with always fresh waves of inscrutability.

It is the glory of God to conceal things,
but the glory of kings to search things out. (Prov 25:2)

It is as though our every capacity to "seek things out" (as in scientific investigation) evokes from the creator God a fresh instance of concealment. This means that wisdom teaching always arrives at provisional awarenesses and explanations, but never at final answers or explanations, and certainly never at "final solutions." As a result we may imagine that the three wisdom materials of Proverbs, Job, and Ecclesiastes constitute something of a "rolling corpus" whereby each piece of literature takes up issues left by the predecessor materials. We may imagine that these three literatures roughly correspond to stages in our acquiring wisdom that runs well beyond knowledge and certitude:

✳ Proverbs: the urge toward moral clarity;
✳ Job: the recognition of the elusiveness of certitude concerning ultimate matters; and
✳ Ecclesiastes: the capacity to dwell responsibly amid inscrutability.

These texts thus provide rich resources for preaching in a society that is wrenched by competing certitudes (liberal and conservative) in which we are wont to know too much. Our contemporary culture is marked by readiness to dwell in settled orthodoxy or reductionist ideology (left or right), and to foreclose on and deny the stubborn granular reality of our lived life. The preacher has the wondrous opportunity, via these texts, to reflect on that stubborn lived reality that will not finally submit to our preferred explanations—religious or scientific, secular or spiritual. The preacher's task, I suggest, is not to settle matters or solve the inscrutability by some form of certitude. It is rather to invite the congregation to dwell in the midst of such palpable mystery that marks our daily life, to dwell there in modest awareness, glad humility, grateful awe, and willingness to embrace our penultimacy (our true destiny), and to live into it responsibly. Such a place for "dwelling" is an emancipatory alternative to the dominant seductions of our world, twin illusions that either conforming orthodoxy or Promethean autonomous selfhood can lead to well-being.

The Book of Proverbs

The book of Proverbs, in large sweep, consists in two sorts of material. First, the long middle sections of the book (10:1–22:16, 25:1–29:27) are made up of two-line sayings that mostly articulate an uncompromising choice between *wise* or *foolish* actions. These two-line sayings are placed in the mouths of elders in the village community who intend to inculcate the young into a sense of moral character that is congruent with the best teaching of the community. That "best teaching" has emerged in the community by long years (generations!) of watchful care about the predictable outcomes of different choices.

This material constitutes practical theology, that is, theology that is profoundly practical. The subject matter of this teaching concerns the most immediate realities of daily life such as money, work, friendship, speech, and food. Charles Taylor has concluded that the radical revaluation of ordinary life was, of course, one of the most fundamental insights of the Jewish-Christian-Islamic religious tradition, that God as creator himself affirms life and being.[1]

Taylor observes that rabbinic Judaism advanced this understanding:

> Perhaps the first important realization of this potentiality in the broader tradition was in Rabbinic Judaism, at the very beginning of the present era, in the Pharisaic idea of a way of living the law which thoroughly permeated the details of everyday life.[2]

Subsequently the Protestant Reformation accented the religious significance of ordinary life in resisting the medieval synthesis of a "higher" religious life:

> The crucial potentiality here was that of conceiving the hallowing of life not as something which takes place only at the limits, as it were, but as a change which can penetrate the full extent of mundane life.[3]

Taylor nicely enlists John Milton, the great Protestant advocate, in affirmation of the ordinary:

> To know
> That which before us lies in daily life
> Is the prime wisdom.[4]

This "prime wisdom" is not found in theological abstraction or speculation, but in observation about how the world really works as God's creation, how the parts are linked together as "cause and effect" or as "deed and consequence." The upshot of such observation is a thick awareness that God's creation is morally coherent, and that daily conduct prospers when it is in sync with that nonnegotiable coherence. Conversely daily life comes to adversity when conduct (behavior and policy) contradict that coherence.

Of course the shape, requirements, and expectations of that moral coherence intrinsic to creation are not completely transparent. They remain hidden and are disclosed only here and there by disciplined observation. For that reason the hard work of the wisdom teachers never ends but continues in the process of discernment. For the same reason, moreover, conclusions reached by wisdom teachers about "cause and effect" or "deed and consequence" do not reach final formulation but are always open to revision in light of fresh discernment. Thus wisdom is not a fixed body of teaching, but a continuing process of alertness.

The preacher has good work to do as a witness to and advocate for the ongoing work of moral discernment. Thus the work of the preacher, via the book of Proverbs, is engagement in moral observation and discernment that aims at character formation for the community of faith that lives in deep tension with the models of character championed by dominant culture.

The other major body of material in the book of Proverbs is the extended poetic articulation of chapters 1–9, wherein "wisdom" is celebrated as the source of life; listeners are urged to attend to wisdom as a guide to life. The play of wisdom in these chapters is most imaginative. On the one hand, wisdom is the accrued teaching of the elders in the community, so that the young are admonished to pay heed to their teaching. On the other hand, however, wisdom becomes an ontological force and agent of the creator God. This is most succinctly voiced in 3:19–20:

The Lord by wisdom founded the earth;
by understanding he established the heavens;
by his knowledge the deeps broke open,
and the clouds drop down the dew.

Wisdom is the means whereby God has ordered the earth, heaven, the deeps below and the clouds above, a conviction echoed in the doxology of Jeremiah in a triple parallelism:

It is he who made the earth by his power,
who established the world by his wisdom,
and by his understanding stretched out the heavens.
(Jer 10:12)

The same imaginative claim for wisdom is more fully voiced in Proverbs 8:22–31 wherein wisdom is said to be the principle of order whereby creation, at the outset, was ordered against chaos. Wisdom is said to be God's first and most intimate partner and agent in the processes of creation. The moral, practical implication of this claim makes clear that congruity with that wise ordering of reality leads to a happy life, but disregard of that teaching ends in death:

For whoever find me finds life and obtains favor from
the Lord;
But those who miss me injure themselves;
All who hate me love death. (8:35–36)

A proper understanding of the book of Proverbs requires that *the pedagogy of daily life* and *the lyrical claim for the ordering of creation* be taken together. The outcome of such interface is that the conduct of daily life is a dramatic performance of the structured reality of creation that cannot be safely violated but that we nonetheless know only in glimpses and traces. The implication is that our daily actions (that on most days seem quite mundane) are in fact an *alliance* we make with the will of the creator or *resistance* we act out against the will of the creator. Consequently daily life is morally serious and urgent. This teaching is against the sentiment (ancient and contemporary) that daily actions do not matter and that there is nothing at stake in the incidental acts of our common life. It might be observed that consumer ideology in our present circumstance is recurring insistence that nothing matters morally in our choices; all that counts is comfort, ease, and convenience. The wisdom tradition insists otherwise, because daily life is inescapably linked to the structure of creation willed by the creator. Because of that linkage, even our most mundane actions and decisions are permeated with moral thickness that we cannot evade.

The fact that wisdom teaching is open-ended and subject to revision in light of new observation brings it close to scientific awareness. Thus the structure of "deed" linked to "consequence" is not unlike scientific investigation to questions like, Does smoking cause cancer? Does vaccination cause autism? The connection of "deed" and "consequence" is (or is not) a given; but our awareness of such connection depends upon steady, attentive observation. The work of the preacher is to nurture a congregation that is morally engaged and morally attentive to daily circumstance, the kind of engagement and attentiveness resisted by consumer numbness. This practice is quite in contrast to authoritarian teaching that imagines that there is a known package of moral certitude. Rather the wisdom tradition (and its practitioners) aims at the formation and maintenance of character so that individual persons are equipped for wise action in always newly emerging circumstance.

We may identify three aspects of this teaching that bears upon character formation.

The wise teachers in the book of Proverbs, moral pedagogues that they are, understand that life consists in making *choices*. They see their children-students as moral agents who will in the course of their lives make many choices. And like every senior, they are concerned that the young should not engage in unwise, irresponsible, self-destructive decisions. The wisdom tradition understands that decisions to be faced in time to come are not the kinds of decisions offered in TV ads in a narcoticized consumer society. They do not worry if one should choose Advil or Tylenol, a Subaru or a Toyota, Crest or Colgate. Those sorts of choices, offered in deceptive advertising, only evidence the limited range of decisions made available to those whose lives are marked as *consumers*.

The young addressed by wisdom, however, are not consumers; they are moral agents who are being shaped as *neighbors*. As a result, they face, in daily life, decisions that are much more serious and much more urgent. The wisdom teachers do not doubt that daily decisions are set in the context of the will and purpose of the creator, so that in the book of Proverbs the didactic two-liners of the middle collections (10:1–22:16 and 25:1–29:27) are in the context of the lyrical affirmations of "wisdom and creation" in Proverbs 1–9. Thus every choice about quotidian matters—about money, friends, work, speech—is a decision that either conforms to the structure of God's creation (and so brings "happiness") or contradicts God's creation (and so brings "death"). The work of the wisdom teachers and preachers is to show that daily decisions are not trivial or incidental, but every decision is an act of choosing life (by acting wisely) or choosing death (by choosing foolishly). We may consider two examples of such instruction.

In 15:17 we are offered one of the "better sayings" of the wisdom tradition wherein the teachers judge one choice is "better" than another.

> Better is a dinner with vegetables where love is
> than fatted ox and hatred with it.

Often the "better" choice is counterintuitive; it does not on the surface seem "better." It is "better" only when it is referred to the will of the creator and the structure of creation. In that light decisions that may look preferable to us are in fact foolish and not better, because they contradict creation as these teachers have been able to discern it.

We might consider that a dinner of "fatted ox" (prime rib) would be better than "a dinner of vegetables"(just salad). When set in the context of the creator God, however, the wisdom tradition sees that a dinner of rich food requires more income, and the pursuit of more income may result in fatigue, and eventually in tension and pressure that evoke family conflict, thus "hatred with it." The alternative is not simply "a dinner of vegetables," for who would choose that? But such a diet more likely permits there to be a table "where love is," because these teachers judge that such a simple lifestyle does not generate such fatigue, tension, and conflict. The wisdom teachers never spell out why "better," but regularly leave a tacit understanding that the choice of a diet (and therefore a lifestyle) is never simply a matter of ease and convenience, but it has all kinds of linkage to the production, distribution, and consumption of food that issues thick questions about neighborliness.

In a second proverb, the wisdom teachers raise issues about socioeconomic inequality that skews the neighborhood:

Those who mock the poor insult their Maker;
those who are glad at calamity will not go unpunished.
(17:5)

It is easy enough to mock the poor. This may be done directly by indifference and disregard. More likely such mocking is accomplished in policy, such as regressive taxation, a low minimum wage, rigged interest rates, and hopeless indebtedness. Such policies of course apparently can be enacted with impunity, because the poor are helpless to retaliate. But, say these teachers, the denigrating of the poor by attitude or policy is not ever in a vacuum. Such mocking takes place in a world where the creator God is regularly attentive to and allied with the poor. Thus policies that willfully cause calamity for the poor (bad health care, poor public schools, work requirements for food stamps, for God's sake!) are not matters of mere economic calculation on the part of the ruling class, but such "mocking" carries with it the seeds of trouble for the perpetrators. In such teaching the poor are situated on the horizon of the creator God, a factor mostly not noticed by the powerful who never make the connection and who imagine that they can do so without cost or risk. The proverb anticipates the belated parable of Matthew 25:31–46!

The wisdom teachers see clearly that every action has a consequence, even if the rich and powerful may think that they can act with impunity. Thus, while these teachers recognize that life is a wide zone of choosing, they also discern that there are *givens* ordered by the creator, outside of which we cannot exercise freedom. The creator has guaranteed connections between choices and consequences that we may not intend, but that are inescapable from the moment of our choosing. For example, one cannot smoke incessantly without high risk of lung cancer.

This is a *given* that science has confirmed through long observation. There was a time when that connection was not yet visible among us, and then disputed, but once discerned has become a reliable conclusion. That is the way the world works! One cannot be lazy and unproductive without ending in disastrous debt. The two-liners in the book of Proverbs constitute a series of such conclusions drawn through long careful observation. These teachers who assert such conclusions know, at their best, that their conclusions will and must be subsequently revised on the basis of continuing observation and the accumulation of new experience.

Interpreters have framed this matter of "choices" and "givens" as "deed and consequence" in which consequences follow inescapably from choices. It is only the foolish who imagine choices without consequences because the creation is morally coherent and the consequences are assured.

Thus in the first case I have cited (15:17), one might wish for a dinner of "fatted ox" . . . "where love is." The wisdom teachers, however, hunch and assert that such an outcome from such a choice is quite unlikely. The odds are very strong that such a meal (and lifestyle) will end in hostility. Thus if one wants an outcome of "where love is," one will wisely choose a menu and lifestyle of "vegetables" that are less demanding and more readily neighborly in simplicity. Here we might usefully refer to the wise work of Wendell Berry who champions "simplicity, diversity, and frugality," and who sees clearly that individual gratification is a self-destructive enterprise of greed. Berry urges that we have "a duty to be old-fashioned," surely an echo of these ancient teachers![5]

In the second of our examples (17:5), it is easy enough to make policies that damage the poor without seeming to run any great political risk. Except, say these teachers, the poor are not alone or abandoned, but live as the "apple" of God's eye. This claim for the poor is unmistakably counterintuitive, because the poor do not seem to be so preferred at all by anyone. This claim insists that a decision to exploit the poor is never with impunity, but soon or late brings with it, characteristically, in this moral universe, strong prospects for calamity for the neighborhood. Notice that the wisdom teachers do not speculate about divine judgment, divine wrath, or even divine initiative. They simply voice confidence in the moral reliability of the creation that cannot be outflanked. Their watchword is "Heed the givens!"

From these texts the preacher is cast as a moral witness to the inescapable connectedness of the world. The task is to help serious people discern the thick choices we make daily without awareness or intentionality. The task is to contend, with some specificity, that the world is morally coherent and that we, in our daily choices, are in fact choosing our futures and the futures of our neighbors. The narcotic of consumerism tends to numb us to the moral hazards of a life lived uncritically in comfort, convenience, and indulgence. Indeed consumer ideology seeks to screen out all the demanding connections that belong to the truth of creation. All such numbness and screening out constitutes an act of foolishness that brings death. Thus, in a large example, our continued mesmerization with fossil fuel is rapidly making our planet unlivable for more and more creaturely species. Such foolishness is justified as a necessity for the continued "growth" of the predatory economy. For good reason Gerhard von Rad terms such foolishness "practical atheism,"[6] an assumption that the world is not ordered and guaranteed by the creator God.

Given the linkage of choices and consequences it would be easy enough to arrive, beyond moral consensus, at moral certitudes that are certifiable so that certain policies and practices would readily and inevitably lead to the good life. This is wisdom as certitude, a great temptation in a scientifically self-confident culture that trusts its capacity to reduce life to exacting formulation.

The wisdom teachers, however, knew better than to reduce their teaching to a packaged moral certitude. For all of their diligence in "seeking things out" (25:2), they also recognized that it is "the glory of God to conceal things." The wisdom teachers recognized and took seriously that there is a hidden quality to the moral coherence of creation that is beyond their mastery, so that wisdom that brings life cannot be fully known and formulated. The result is that our best judgments concerning the nature of lived reality (moral or scientific) are subject to fresh articulation in light of new awareness. The requirement of that fresh awareness is respect for the deep mystery of life, humility in our best judgment, and readiness for reformulation as evidence demands. Thus "new occasions teach new duties," writes James Russell Lowell in his poem "Once to Every Man and Nation."[7] So "new occasions" arise when a new experience occurs that was not previously available. Such new occasions assign to us the "new duty" of reformulation and abandonment of old certitudes. New awareness requires radical reformulation. Thus, for example, we have learned, over grudging time, new ways about LGBTQ orientation and have adjusted our certitudes in appropriate ways. It is no wonder that "God is still speaking" has become one mantra for those new truths. Who knows, for example, when we might come to understand the high cost of white supremacy and enact policies of reparation that are indispensible for a just neighborhood? We live in a time of such insistent "new duties."

Gerhard von Rad has discerningly identified six proverbs in which these teachers acknowledge a capacity for wonder concerning the ongoing mystery of creation governed by the creator beyond all of our explanatory categories.[8]

> The plans of the mind belong to mortals,
> but the answer of the tongue is from the Lord.
> All one's ways may be pure in one's own eyes,
> but the Lord weighs the spirit. (16:1–2)

> The human mind plans the way,
> but the Lord directs the steps. (16:9)

> The human mind may devise many plans,
> but it is the purpose of the Lord that will be established. (19:21)

> All of our steps are ordered by the Lord;
> how then can we understand our own ways? (20:24)

> All deeds are right in the sight of the doer,
> but the Lord weighs the heart. (21:2)

> No wisdom, no understanding, no counsel, can avail
> against the Lord.
> The horse is made ready for the day of battle,
> but victory belongs to the Lord. (21:30–31)

These wisdom teachers knew that the ways of God, in God's freedom, run well beyond our best certitudes; they took seriously new observations that required revised teaching. This freedom on God's part means that the creator is not a prisoner to the "deed–consequence" structure of creation that God has ordained but can act in freedom and surprise beyond explanation or expectation. Thus in 19:21 the purpose of God will, on occasion, rush beyond the best of human planning, sometimes to good outcome, sometimes not.

The last of these references concerns military planning and practice:

The horse is made ready for the day of battle,
but the victory belongs to the Lord. (21:31)

Perhaps US involvement in Vietnam is an instance of the truth of this maxim. The US military did its best planning, strong mobilization, and intense rationalization for the war. Who knew that the intent of our great military apparatus could be thwarted by stubborn indigenous resistance? Indeed we might expect these wisdom teachers to anticipate the belated judgment of Robert McNamara, US Secretary of Defense, in the documentary *The Fog of War*. It is that "fog," perhaps God-sent (see Isa 19:14; Lev 26:36–38), that precluded US victory. Victory was somehow assigned differently, US "superiority" notwithstanding. The outcome of that war might invite greater prudence and humility in future military ventures.

In the end the wisdom teachers understood that our best moral reasoning is always linked to what we cannot control. Thus this moral instruction is not aimed at final conclusions or certitudes. It is aimed, rather, at character that can self-critically and reflectively engage in the urgent processes of moral reasoning in newly emerging circumstance. In a culture wherein responsibility is flattened to ideological passion and wherein relationships of fidelity are reduced to commodity, moral reasoning of this kind is urgent. The preacher can lead in this enterprise that is not heavy-handed or authoritarian, but is passionately committed to character formation that persists in the midst of thin, instrumental reasoning. Such moral reasoning is not embarrassed by the claim that the holiness of God is not contained in our preferred ideology. It insists that the intractable insistences of the created order are not negated by the "fog."

For good reason Erhard Gerstenberger long ago suggested that Proverbs 3:7–8 might be taken as an epitome for the book of Proverbs:

> Do not be wise in your own eyes;
> fear the Lord, and turn away from evil.
> It will be healing for your flesh
> and a refreshment for your body.

This mandate yields three imperatives:

The first, "do not be wise," warns against excessive certitude and confidence in one's own judgments, imagining that we know more than we do.

The second, "fear the Lord," affirms that genuine understanding begins with an awareness of the decisive reality of God; God's holy intentionality for the creation will prevail.

The third, "turn away from evil," warns about the seductive alternatives that may talk us out of moral responsibility and so compromise moral character.

The anticipated outcome of verse 8 has the ring of consequence for the deeds of verse 7. The three "deeds" of verse 7 (do not be wise, fear the Lord, turn away from evil), yield the outcomes of verse 8: healing and refreshment (drink!), that is, well-being. Conversely,

> Folly is a lack of order in a man's innermost being, a lack which defies all instruction. . . . Folly is practical atheism.[9]

The Book of Job

The book of Proverbs provides the baseline for the book of Job. The *premise* of the book of Job is that there is, in God's creation, a "deed–consequence" structure that is reliably guaranteed by God. As a result of that reliable order, human creatures choose their own futures by their ethical choices and conduct. The *problem* of the book of Job is that the premise of a reliable order is finally not true to lived experience. Thus the work of the preacher is to engage that *premise* and to probe that *problem*.

It is an easy temptation for the preacher to lift out of context specific verses from the book of Job in a way that disregards the grand dramatic plot of the book. Among favorites for such extraction are two verses:

> The Lord gave, and the Lord has taken away; blessed be the name of the Lord. (1:21)

And with a nod to Handel's *Messiah:*

> For I know that my Redeemer lives,
> and that at the last he will stand on the earth. (19:25)

Such disregard of context, of course, ill serves the text or the congregation.

The more difficult task for the preacher is to engage the dramatic plot of the book. That task is difficult for two reasons. First, the plot itself is dense, tangled, and unresolved. Second and more immediately, the sermonic practice of the church limits the preacher's capacity to deal with an extended text that must be taken up over time without rush. Engagement with the plot of the book of Job cannot be done summarily. The work, rather, must be unfolded in a paced and disciplined way in order to allow the congregation to enter into the work of the drama as we might in any good theater performance.

Thus at the outset the preacher must have clearly in purview the plot of the book that is offered in three unequal parts. The book begins in a simple, well-ordered folk village in chapters 1–2. It continues in the long conflicted dramatic exchange of 3:1–42:6, and it ends in the resolve of 42:7–17. I can think of three ways in which to engage its dramatic structure and movement.

First, the dramatic movement of the book is a clear example of my argument that the book of Psalms can be understood as a movement from a life of *orientation* in which all is well ordered, through a season of *disorientation* in which all old certitudes are seen to be in jeopardy, to a *new orientation* that is a fresh gift from God. The book of Job carries the fictive character Job exactly through that sequence. Job is drawn from a simple life of well-being, "blameless and upright," through an ordeal of disorienting disputatious restlessness in the presence of God's awesome holiness, finally to arrive at a life "full of days" of blessing (42:17).

Second, Paul Ricoeur (whose work lies behind my plotting of the book of Psalms) has proposed that a life of faithful awareness moves from a *"pre-critical"* understanding in which common, taken-for-granted social assumptions are accepted without question, to a *"critical"* awareness in which old assumptions are addressed with unblinking skepticism, and finally arrives at a *"post-critical"* sensibility in which what has been critically regarded with "suspicion" is now retrieved and reembraced, but now with a knowing awareness.

My sense of the movement of "pre-critical–critical–post-critical" sensibility perforce *pertains to Scripture*. Thus the preacher can in gentle ways help the congregation to move from a pre-critical sense of the Bible ("Moses wrote it all"), to a critical awareness of the passionate advocacy of various voices in the text, to post-critical recognition of Scripture as revelatory and authoritative. Alongside that learning about Scripture, the preacher can also assist members of the church to a growing *sense of self.* That sense of self might move from a pre-critical self ("what my mother intended me to be"), to a critical self in which one becomes aware of the complexity of the "many selves of the self," and finally to a post-critical recognition: given who I am, God and my mother love me nonetheless. Alongside that movement concerning Scripture and self, the same dynamic pertains concerning *the reality of God*, a dynamics that is the work of spiritual maturation. Thus God taken pre-critically is as straightforward as the one given in the creeds. Taken critically, "God" may be reduced, à la Feuerbach, to human projection. But taken post-critically, God is revealed in and through and beyond our best criticism. The work is to enable the congregation to track these processes in its own maturing discernment.

Third, my brilliant student Tod Linafelt has suggested that the dynamic structure of the book of Job is not unlike the structure of *The Wizard of Oz.* In the beginning Dorothy is in "Kansas," a safe simple place that is monochromatic. So Job, "blameless and upright," lives in the safe, simple place of Oz. As Dorothy falls asleep, she enters the rich vibrant, multicolored world of Oz. It is a dream-world of imagination that teems with characters and prospects not on the horizon of "Kansas." So Job, once his silenced piety is broken, enters a risky, dangerous world of dialogic interaction that is filled with dispute and is presided over by a creator God who is awesome and inexplicable, and who refuses to be contained in the categories of safe, simple "Kansas." In the end Dorothy returns to "Kansas." But when she returns to "Kansas" that is still monochromatic, she is in a very different place. The dream-world is transformational. Job returns to his old place, chastened, saddened, and sobered, but still pious. The dialogic world is transformative for him! In Dorothy's story the beginning and end in "Kansas" are brief with all the space given over to Oz. So also for Job.

Each of these taxonomies serves the same intent:

Job 1–2	Job 3:1–42:6	Job 42:7–17
orientation	disorientation	new orientation
pre-critical	critical	post-critical
Kansas	Oz	Kansas

They invite us to new waves of awareness and honesty that may culminate a fresh engagement with the holiness of God. It is clear in the book of Job that we cannot do without the taken-for-granted world of the book of Proverbs that issues in "blameless and upright." It is equally clear, however, that we remain in the book of Proverbs to our great peril, because the reality of our lives is much more complex, thick, and risky than is allowed there. The preacher can be a guide and leader for entrance into the complex, thick, and risky reality of truthfulness where we may meet God in profound ways that are not yet on the horizon of "Kansas." We cannot, however, sustain that risky complexity forever and are glad, soon or late, to return, albeit sobered, to "Kansas."

The preacher can invite the congregation to dwell for a while in the innocent land of Oz (Job 1–2). Perhaps the work there is to bring to consciousness the reality of how much we count on (and even absolutize) our sense of deeds–consequences concerning money, sexuality, and all manner of things. Unless and until we are conscious of this, we are unlikely to engage the book of Job in a serious way. Thus the church is characteristically a convinced lobbyist for deeds–consequences in its advocacy for an unbending morality. The other reality Job had to face here is the fact that in the mystery of God all that he cherished is losable. Thus in the text of Job, chapter 1 patiently lets us experience and affirm all that Job had possessed and then requires us to attend to the slow unbearable process of loss:

* Oxen, donkeys, and servants: "I alone have escaped to tell you" (v. 15).
* Sheep and servants: "I alone have escaped to tell you" (v. 16).
* Camels and servants: "I alone have escaped to tell you" (v. 17).
* Sons, daughters, young people: "I alone have escaped to tell you" (v. 19).

Only a messenger remains, but no oxen, donkeys, or servants. Only a messenger is left, but no sheep or servants. Only a messenger is left, but no camels or servants. Only a messenger is left, but no sons or daughters, no "young people."

The loss evokes questions that pastors hear all the time: "Why me? What did I do wrong?" "Would that it had been me instead of my son/daughter!" This "blameless and upright" man is pushed well beyond his comfort zone as we all will be, soon or late. And then begins the great struggle that cannot be avoided that Job must adjudicate. On the one hand, his piety persists. He will still bless God and not accuse God (1:21–22). He will not sin with his lips and must rebuke his wife (2:10). At this point he does not anticipate that very soon he himself will join in his wife's honesty before God.

On the other hand, however, he is not left alone in his terrible grief. He has friends who have not abandoned him (2:11). They wept with him. They kept silent with him. They waited with him. That long, unbearable wait in such attentive company moved Job beyond conventional piety. Left alone he might have settled for denial. But he could finally not end in denial. He had to speak. Thus the preacher may imagine that as we live in a culture of immense loss we are in various places between denial and honesty. If we (or Job) remain in silent accepting denial, the book of Job must end after two chapters. But of course the point is that it cannot end there. The waiting in attentive company brought him to speech. The task of the preacher is to break the terrible silence of loss and unleash relentless honesty without which there will be no future. It is his silent attentive friends—weeping and waiting—who make a future possible via speech:

> We share each other's woe, our mutual burdens bear;
> And often for each other flows the sympathizing tear.
> ("Blest Be the Tie That Binds," *The United Methodist Hymnal* 557; see Rom 12:15)

The preacher can legitimate a move into the dread-filled dialogue that makes a way out of no way (3:1–42:6). The way forward is through dispute. It is a dispute, likely internal, about pious acceptance of loss or honest rage voiced at high risk before God. That internal struggle is here given visible dramatic performance so that the preacher may dare to line out in public the work that often remains hidden and which is inescapably undertaken by so many carriers of loss.

The friends give voice to pious acceptance that echoes the confident deed–consequence structure of the book of Proverbs.

On the surface their speeches are not very interesting or compelling. But there is more to their speech than simple acceptance of given structure. Davis Hankins has proposed that in fact these speeches also function as consolation for Job,[10] thus speech that accompanies the waiting of the friends in 2:11–13. The consolation given to Job is that along with confident affirmation of retribution, they also recognize an awesome indeterminacy that undermines that confidence. There is hope in God-given indeterminacy. Eliphaz is in fact not an insistent moral teacher but a one whose work of consolation is "not unlike a kind of talk therapy" that exhibits the flexibility of a pastor or an analyst engaged in dream interpretation. Eliphaz knows that too much certainty is foolish; he remembers from Proverbs that God is not prisoner to any system of payback.

It is perhaps this indeterminacy that allows Job sufficient courage to speak. He will not swallow his pain and loss for the sake of his piety. He dares utter honesty before God what amounts to an accusation against God because of God's injustice:

> Though I am blameless he would prove me perverse.
> "I am blameless; I don't know myself;
> I loathe myself.
> It is all one; therefore I say,
> he destroys both the blameless and the wicked.
> When disaster brings sudden death,
> he mocks the calamity of the innocent." (9:20–23)

According to Job, God fails to uphold and guarantee the deed–consequence structure of moral coherence so that there is no good payback for pious conduct. Job's chutzpah comes to full expression in his final defiant utterance before God:

Oh, that I had someone to hear me! . . .
Oh, that I had the indictment written by my adversary!
Surely I would carry it on my shoulder;
I would bind it on me like a crown;
I would give him account of all my steps;
like a prince I would approach him. (31:35–37)

Job is not humbled, silenced, or intimidated. He claims the full authority that is given him by his acknowledged loss and pain. He has no doubt that he merits a response from God who all this time has been silent. He waits in his innocence.

But then YHWH answers! (God has not been called by this covenantal name YHWH since the opening narrative. We are back in the land of covenant!) The first wonder of the drama of Job is that God answers (beginning in 38:1). But the second wonder of the book of Job is that God's answer to Job is no answer at all. God never acknowledges what Job has said. God has no obligation to dispute with Job or to defend any deed–consequence system. In the speeches of God that follow, Job is confronted by the raw holiness of God who is not subject to or confined by the best reasoning of Job, or the best wisdom of his friends, or the best confidence of the book of Proverbs.

The preacher's task in this unbearably demanding exchange is to put on full exhibit the truthfulness of ambiguity. Job wishes for God's presence but also finds God oppressive and hopes for God's absence. God answers Job but answers in dismissive holiness. So these two unequal partners meet at last. They do not meet, however, in any conventional way or in a way that admits of resolution. They meet in an ambiguous awareness that they must, so to speak, coexist in the world together, unequal in power but unavoidable to each other. The hope of the text—and the work of the preacher—is to witness beyond resolution or explanation to aching mystery that some interpreters take to be "the sublime." The sublime is an unutterable awe that defies exposition. Job has broken beyond all conventional wisdom to look boldly into the face of holy mystery. He is a daring subversive:

> No wonder the friends have nothing else to say. They speak a language of sanity in a presumptively sane world. Job speaks a language bordering on madness in a world turned upside down. Job's language, however, has the quality of a dare or a provocation. He has mastered one of the possible languages of subversive resistance in a totalitarian world.[11]

That subversion takes the form of near-madness that refuses explanatory sanity. We must, nonetheless, go there in the face of immense loss, because anything less rings false. Job's final utterance in 42:1–6 is deeply enigmatic. It is easy and conventional to take his words as submission to God. That, however, is the gift of reassuring translation. The statement in 42:6 is in fact coy, playful, and unsettled. It accommodates neither the breathtaking force of God, nor the "sanity" of Job's friends, nor the indignation of Job's protest. We are best led by the eloquent discernment of Sam Balentine:

> Having listened in as God celebrates the virtues of Behemoth and Leviathan, Job now understands that there is indeed a place in God's world for creatures that refuse to submit to forces that would rob them of their dignity by reducing them to slaves to wanton misery. Like them, God has endowed human beings with power and

responsibility for their domains. They too have been created to be fierce and unbridled opponents of injustice, sometimes *with* God, sometimes *against* God, even if it means they will lose the fight. . . . As near equals of God, their destiny is to live at the dangerous intersection between the merely human and the supremely divine. When human beings dare to live out this mandate, their appearance before God as "dust and ashes" confirms their heritage as faithful descendents of Abraham. They may be sure that if they dare to live faithfully into their legacy, they will find themselves standing before a Creator who awaits and desires their arrival. They may speak words of praise; they may speak words of curse. They may also risk moving beyond these levels of discourse to speak words of resistance and protest. . . . But they must not be silent, for silence is unworthy of those who have stood in the divine presence and have learned that creation has been entrusted to them, because they are a "little lower than God."[12]

The drama has been pushed as far as this dramatist can imagine. We are left unsettled as the engagement remains unresolved.

The preacher's task in the third concluding part of the book of Job is to ease the congregation back into the real world, back to "Kansas," after the daring exploration (42:7–17). Thus Job may return to the safe, simple world of Job 1–2 where it made sense to be "blameless and upright." He does not, however, return as the same person. His return is like a return after being at a theater performance that jolts one's assumptions. Or it is like a return after a daring sermon that has jolted old thought. It is like a return after recognizing how flimsy are the old assurances.

Job receives a new assurance, one that conventional wisdom might not have expected. God's anger is toward the friends, perhaps for knowing too much or settling too easily, a temptation for anyone who is in the "explanation business." By contrast Job received divine commendation (vv. 7–8). More than that, Job is to pray for his friends. The outcome: "The prayer of the righteous is powerful and effective" (Jas 5:16). The outcome of Job's prayer is that God accepts Job's prayer for the three disapproved friends.

Job goes back home. All is restored. Davis Hankins has seen that Job returns to his community to take up his erstwhile role in the maintenance of the community:

> The most significant ethical aspect of the prose conclusion is its shift of focus from a subject-centered concern with Job's understanding, activities, and obedience, to Job's role in what constitutes and maintains the cultural, legal, and religious institutions of the community. . . . The prose conclusion, however, shifts the focus toward the community and toward Job's role in what constitutes and maintains the collective.[13]

Job is able to move past his personal anguish to notice, yet again, the neighborhood for which he had cared so generously in the past (see 31:1–24, 38–40). That notice is what may happen, at best, when we face uncommon personal loss. Soon or late we return to a proper place in the community, unless of course we are not able or willing to do so. Job is both willing and able; he ends "full of days" (42:17).

This ending is reassuring. But this character ending "full of days" is also full of durable pain. "The Lord restored the fortunes of Job" (42:10). He is more blessed at the end than at the beginning. Now he has an inventory of possessions that overflows:

> Fourteen thousand sheep!
> Six thousand camels!
> One thousand yoke of oxen!
> One thousand donkeys!
> Seven sons!
> Three daughters! (We know their names and they are
>   beautiful!). (vv. 12–15)

We can imagine that Job receives back his social prominence, for which he had grieved in chapter 30. Maybe he staged more festivals. Maybe be offered lavish dinners, was highly respected, and basked in the gratitude of the community.

Emil Fackenheim, however, has noticed that while Job had new sons and daughters, he could not and did not retrieve his sons and daughters from chapter 1. Indeed, with an allusion to the Shoah, Fackenheim allows that Job had lost *six million sons and daughters* that remain beyond retrieval. We may imagine that Job, at the end of a busy day of social interaction, was alone at night. We may imagine, moreover, that he wept alone in the night. He wept his durable loss, not because he did not love his new progeny, but because they could never be fully adequate substitutes. They could not be!

By the end of the book, Job's "suffering was great," just as it was great early on (2:13). He has received some consolation from his friends and from God, and he has witnessed restoration. That reality, however, does not erase his great suffering that he now must manage to live with. The preacher stands in the midst of that reality. The preacher legitimates the anguish of Job. The preacher reiterates the wise company of the friends.

The preacher attests the undomesticated holiness of God that goes beyond Job's loss. And the preacher stands alongside a congregation full of Jobs who are at various places in the script. The preacher rejoices with those who rejoice in the daytime. The preacher weeps with those who weep in the night, knowing that "weeping may linger for the night" (Ps 30:5). Job was "full of days," but surely he was "full of nights" as well.

The Book of Ecclesiates

The third piece of wisdom literature in the Old Testament, Ecclesiastes, is in terms of a historical-critical judgment well removed from the book of Job, by perhaps as much as three centuries later. For our purposes, however, we may imagine that Ecclesiastes arises in the wake of the book of Job. We have seen operative in the book of Job immense theological energy and imagination capable of pushing the envelope of the unthinkable. When we arrive at Ecclesiastes it is as though that energy and imagination are largely absent. Now the voice of the wisdom tradition ("the preacher"), in the midst of Ptolemaic imperial control, sounds a tone of exhaustion that tilts toward resignation. Thus the book may be a rich resource for the contemporary preacher who must make contact with world-weary folk who conclude that the world is too complex for moral management and too intransigent for anything more than occasional amelioration. It may be that Hellenistic reasonableness has gained force in a way that crowds out the urgency and daring of Jewish hope-filled utterance. For whatever reason, the hope that wisdom may "search things out" (Prov 25:1) no longer evokes much interest, energy, or courage. Here things have been sorted out and found to be less than affirming or generative. There is no energy on offer to do more by way of insistent probe. Thus we get, in Ecclesiastes, an inventory of failed hopes for work, self-indulgence, money, and desire. None of these will arrive at a good outcome:

> Everything that confronts them is vanity, since the same fate comes to all, to the righteous and the wicked, to the good and the evil, to the clean and the unclean, to those who sacrifice and those who do not sacrifice. As are the good, so are the sinners; those who swear are like those who shun an oath. (9:1–3)

For good reason Jack Miles includes Ecclesiastes among "the books of silence," that is, Old Testament books that do not make much of God and who consequently seem none the wiser concerning any ultimate good.

> What is the meaning of the long twilight of the Hebrew Bible, its ten closing books of silence? This twilight is not followed by darkness: God does not die. But he never again intervenes in human affairs, and by accumulating implication, no further intervention is expected of him.[14]

The writer does not expect anything. Thus he anticipates the very modest asking of the church as it seeks that the Spirit of God may descend in a time in the nineteenth century when the church was not able to voice robust expectation of God:

> I ask no dream, no prophet ecstasies,
> No sudden rending of the veil of clay,
> No angel visitant, no opening skies.
> (Spirit of God, *The United Methodist Hymnal* 500)

The last line of the verse concludes with a very modest asking:

Take the dimness of my heart away.

But our writer does not ask even that. He seems willing to settle for dimmed vision of reality that is closed over; there is no Joban indignation, no Joban wonderment or challenge, no energy, no imagination, no defiant buoyancy. The world-weary teacher who speaks here represents an important challenge to the contemporary preacher who is tempted, on occasion, to stand with and alongside the world-weary as the preacher sees and know how little we change and how deeply reluctant we are about alternative possibilities. This speaker has long since given up any characteristically Jewish conviction about being able to make claims against God's holiness, a conviction still important in the drama of Job.

Of course the contemporary preacher must do more than acknowledge this world-weariness. I suggest that there are at least three notes (maybe more) that are on offer that still ring true, even in the face of such resignation.

First, in this text it is not so dark and hopeless that all cats appear to be gray. There can still be moral distinctions. Thus even here we are given a series of "better sayings" that remember from old wisdom that we are still to be morally alert and discriminating:

Better is a handful with quiet
than two handfuls with toil, and a chasing after wind.
    (4:6)

Better is a poor but wise youth
than an old but foolish king who will no longer take
    advice. (4:13)

A good name is better than precious ointment,
and the day of death than the day of birth.
It is better to go to the house of mourning
than to the house of feasting;
for this is the end of everyone,
and the living will lay it to heart.
Sorrow is better than laughter,
for by sadness of countenance the heart is made
glad. . . .
It is better to hear the rebuke of the wise
than to hear the song of fools. (7:1–5)

(It is possible to read this last saying as an anticipation of the wisdom saying of Jesus in Luke 6:20–26. Jesus commends weeping and mourning now in prospect of later laughter and joy.) To be sure, there is a kind of sobriety about these claims, but they make clear that even in a world of exhausted morality, we are not excused from discerning moral responsibility. There are still decisions to be made that matter. And wisdom may be a teacher for that:

Wisdom is as good as an inheritance,
and advantage to those who see the sun.
For the protection of wisdom is like the protection of
money,
and the advantage of knowledge is that wisdom gives
life to the one who possesses it. (7:11–12)

The writer continues to value such a legacy ("inheritance") even as he recognizes that in a world of moral indifference, wisdom does not count for much:

Wisdom is better than might;
yet the poor man's wisdom is despised,
and his words are not heeded.
The quiet words of the wise are more to be heeded
than the shouting of a ruler among fools.
Wisdom is better than weapons of war,
but one bungler destroys much good. (9:16–18)

Even in his belated world, the writer is not very far from the earlier admonition:

Get wisdom, get insight;
do not forget nor turn away from the words of my
mouth. (Prov 4:5)

Second, even in a world of inescapable "fate," there are still proximate, penultimate joys, and we should make the most of them. The sobriety of "one fate for all" should not lead away from a capacity for joy in the gifts of creation:

There is nothing better for mortals than to eat and drink,
and find enjoyment in their toil. (2:24)

Go, eat your bread with enjoyment,
and drink your wine with a merry heart;
for God has long ago approved what you do. (9:7)

This honest teacher is not world-rejecting but is vigorously world-affirming. He knows that this is still God's good creation that teems with gifts that are given to human persons and human community, even when we cannot see the ultimate outcome of existence. Do not be devoured by such ultimate obscurity but live well, joyfully, and gratefully in the present. This is an echo of the early wisdom tradition that invites to a well-lived life. Even in a context of resignation, one rightly can count one's blessings and live in well-being. Such joy, to be sure, is not an escape from responsibility.

Third, after resignation and even cynicism, the writer draws a conclusion that is resonate with the claims of old wisdom:

> This is the end of the matter; all has been heard. Fear God, and keep his commandments; that is the whole duty of everyone. (12:13)

This preacher situates himself in the company of the "sayings of the wise" and continues the task of "weighing, studying, and arranging" proverbs. The core imperatives of this final admonition are only two. First, "fear God." This preacher has not strayed from the old adage that "the fear of the Lord is the beginning of wisdom" (Prov 1:7). Such awed response to God is not a conclusion but a premise of a good life. The second imperative concerns obedience to the commandments, so that wisdom, in the centuries following Ezra, coalesced with Torah commandments. The imperative does not specify, but we may judge that the entire corpus of Torah is intended, along "with interpretation," as in the work of Ezra (Neh 8:7–8). This preacher surely recognized the dynamic character of Torah as he knew that wisdom teaching is always in process. The final clause of the verse is a summons to duty. But the Hebrew is even more comprehensive. "This is the *all* of the human person." The sum of human existence is adherence to the commandment!

It may be that this summation is a late editorial add-on to the corpus of the book that seeks to overcome the weary resignation of it early parts. This resignation is in purview as late as 12:8. Once more:

> Vanity of vanities, says the Teacher, all is vanity. (12:8)

We can allow, however, that the preacher, having affirmed agnosticism of ultimate things, has a real passion for penultimate Torah responsibility. Thus the contemporary preacher need not be entangled in ultimate perplexities, but can instead give heed to the realities of the day that are demanding enough. It may be that the final two verses open to an eschatological prospect: God ultimately will sort out "good or evil." This conclusion attests that even in a world of hidden fate, we are not off the hook of living responsibly in the meantime.

Taken together, these three summary points attest that *moral judgments* can be made; they may be made in acts of *life-affirming joy*. Such judgments, moreover, may indeed cohere with the shape of creation and *the will of the creator*. The rest is left in hands of the inscrutable sovereign. The future is hidden; it is not, however, in free fall; it is held in the hands of the creator who has not resigned, even in the midst of our resignation.

NOTES

Chapter 1: Preaching from the Torah: Genesis

1. See Matthew Fox, *Original Blessing: A Primer on Creation Spirituality* (New York: Putnam, 2000).
2. On the continuing contemporary problem of chosenness, see Todd Gitlin and Liel Leibovitz, *The Chosen Peoples: America, Israel, and the Ordeal of Divine Election* (New York: Simon & Schuster, 2010).
3. See Daniel L. Smith, *The Religion of the Landless: The Social Context of the Babylonian Exile* (Bloomington, IN: Meyer Stone, 1989); Daniel L. Smith-Christopher, *A Biblical Theology of Exile* (Minneapolis: Fortress, 2002).
4. Jon D. Levenson (*Inheriting Abraham: The Legacy of the Patriarch in Judaism, Christianity, and Islam* [Princeton: Princeton University Press, 2012]) has explored the complex, problematic matter of the way in which the three book religions share the legacy of Abraham. Levenson resists any easy accommodation among these traditions in their very different interpretive practices.
5. Robert W. Jenson, *Canon and Creed*, Interpretation (Louisville: Westminster John Knox, 2010), 120.
6. Michael Fishbane, *Sacred Attunement: A Jewish Theology* (Chicago: University of Chicago Press, 2008), 126.
7. Sarah Coakley, *God, Sexuality, and the Self: An Essay "On the Trinity,"* (Cambridge: Cambridge University Press, 2013).
8. Helder Camara, *Spiral of Violence* (Denville, NJ: Dimension, 1971).

9. There are now a number of studies of violence on the part of God in the Old Testament: Matthias Beier, *A Violent God-Image: An Introduction to the Work of Eugen Drewermann* (New York: Continuum, 2006); Jerome F. D. Creach, *Violence in Scripture*, Interpretation (Louisville: Westminster John Knox, 2013); Michael G. Long, ed., *Christian Peace and Nonviolence: A Documentary History* (Maryknoll, NY: Orbis, 2011); Patricia M. McDonald, *God and Violence: Biblical Resources for Living in a Small World* (Scottsdale, PA: Herald, 2004); Eric A. Seibert, *The Violence of Scripture: Overcoming the Old Testament's Troubling Legacy* (Minneapolis: Fortress, 2012); Eric A. Seibert, *Disturbing Divine Behavior: Troubling Old Testament Images of God* (Minneapolis: Fortress, 2009); Jeremy Young, *The Violence of God and the War on Terror* (London: Darton, Longman & Todd, 2007). Among these, the best one is that of Creach.

10. Gerhard von Rad, *Genesis: A Commentary*, OTL (Philadelphia: Westminster, 1972).

11. Martin Buber (*Right and Wrong* [London: SCM, 1952], 34–52) explored the way in which the "heart" is narrated in Psalm 73.

12. Gerhard von Rad, *Old Testament Theology I* (New York: Harper & Row, 1962) 165–75; Claus Westermann, *The Promises to the Fathers: Studies on the Patriarchal Narratives* (Philadelphia: Fortress, 1980).

13. Jon D. Levenson, *Creation and the Persistence of Evil: The Jewish Drama of Divine Omnipotence* (San Francisco: Harper & Row, 1988), 151, 153.

14. Leon R. Kass, *The Beginning of Wisdom: Reading Genesis* (New York: Free Press, 2003), 569.

Chapter 2: Preaching from the Torah: The Tale of Moses

1. Treatment of the narrative as paradigmatic is made clear by Erich Voegelin, *Israel and Revelation: Order and History 1* (Baton Rouge: Louisiana State University, 1956).

2. Robert Jay Lifton (*Witness to an Extreme Century: A Memoir* [New York: Free Press, 2011], 67–68, 381) has fully exposited the reality of totalism.

3. See Leon R. Kass, *The Beginning of Wisdom: Reading Genesis* (New York: Free Press, 2003), 569–70.

4. On the disqualification of the poor that subjects them to violence, see Gary A. Haugen and Victor Bautros, *The Locust Effect: Why the End of Poverty Requires the End of Violence* (Oxford: Oxford University Press, 2014).

5. On the cruciality of that voice being heard, see John Paul Lederach and Angela Jill Lederach, *When Blood and Bones Cry Out: Journeys through the Soundscape of Healing and Reconciliation* (Oxford: Oxford University Press, 2010).

6. See Enrique Dussel, *Ethics of Liberation in the Age of Globalization and Exclusion* (Durham: Duke University Press, 2013), 242–44.

7. See Martha C. Nussbaum, *The Clash Within: Democracy, Religious Violence, and India's Future* (Cambridge, MA: Belknap, 2007), 336–37.

8. David Brooks, "A Long Obedience," *The New York Times* (April 15, 2014), A21. See as well Bruce Feiler, *America's Prophet: Moses and the American Story* (New York: William Morrow, 2009).

9. Walter Brueggemann, "The Countercommands of Sinai," in *Disruptive Grace: Reflections on God, Scripture, and the Church*, ed. Carolyn J. Sharp (Minneapolis: Fortress, 2011), 75–92.

10. Walter Brueggemann, *Sabbath as Resistance: Saying No to the Culture of Now* (Louisville: Westminster John Knox, 2014).

11. Brooks, "Long Obedience," A21.

12. See Bernhard W. Anderson, "Exodus Typology in Second Isaiah," in *Israel's Prophetic Heritage: Essays in Honor of James Muilenburg*, ed. Bernhard W. Anderson and Walter Harrelson (New York: Harper, 1962), 177–95. In a later article ("Exodus and Covenant in Second Isaiah and the Prophetic Tradition," in *Magnalia Dei: The Mighty Acts of God; Essays on the Bible and Archeology in Memory of G. Ernest Wright*, ed. Frank Moore Cross et al. [Garden City, NY: Doubleday,

1976], 339–60), Anderson has shown how Second Isaiah uses not only the typology of exodus but that of covenant as well.

13. See Richard Horsley, *Jesus and Empire: The Kingdom of God and the New World Disorder* (Minneapolis: Fortress, 2003).

14. Brigitte Kahl, *Galatians Re-imagined: Reading with the Eyes of the Vanquished* (Minneapolis: Fortress, 2010).

15. R. Alan Streett, *Subversive Meals: Eating the Lord's Supper under Roman Domination during the First Century* (Eugene, OR: Wipf & Stock, 2013).

Chapter 3: Preaching from the Prophets

1. Francis X. Clines, "Seamus Heaney, Poet of 'Silent Things,'" *The New York Times* (August 31, 2013), A14.

2. This is a canonical judgment that is against both the still-dominant critical consensus of Wellhausen and the more recent propensity among scholars to date everything quite late.

3. See Walter Brueggemann, "The Countercommands of Sinai," in *Disruptive Grace: Reflections on God, Scripture, and the Church*, ed. Carolyn J. Sharp (Minneapolis: Fortress, 2011), 75–92.

4. Claus Westermann, *The Promise to the Fathers: Studies on the Patriarchal Narratives* (Philadelphia: Fortress, 1980); David J. A. Clines, *The Theme of the Pentateuch*, JSOTSup 10 (Sheffield: University of Sheffield, 1978).

5. Gerhard von Rad, *Studies in Deuteronomy* (Chicago: Regnery, 1953).

6. John Paul Lederach and Angela Jill Lederach, *When Blood and Bones Cry Out: Journey through the Soundscape of Healing and Reconciliation* (Oxford: University of Oxford Press, 2010), 67. I am glad to thank Peter Block for this reference.

7. Lederach and Lederach, *When Blood and Bones Cry Out*, 73, where the authors quote Jacques Attali.

8. Lederach and Lederach, *When Blood and Bones Cry Out*, 154–55 (emphasis added).

9. Lederach and Lederach, *When Blood and Bones Cry Out*, 173, where the authors quote Oumar Farouk Sesay.

10. Margalit Fox, "He Wove Irish Strife and Soil into Silken Verse," *The News York Times* (August 31, 2013), B12.

Chapter 4: Preaching from the Psalms

1. Gerhard von Rad, *Old Testament Theology I: The Theology of Israel's Historical Traditions* (New York: Harper & Row, 1962), 355–417.

2. John Calvin, *Institutes of the Christian Religion*, LCC 20 (Philadelphia: Westminster, 1960), 35–39.

3. For an echo of this perspective, see Peter L. Berger, *A Rumor of Angels: Modern Society and the Rediscovery of the Supernatural* (Garden City, NY: Anchor, 1970).

4. Jonathan Haidt, *The Righteous Mind: Why Good People Are Divided by Politics and Religion* (New York: Pantheon, 2012).

5. George Stroup (*Before God* [Grand Rapids: Eerdmans, 2004]) has offered a penetrating exposition of the phrase.

6. The point is effectively made by Harold Fisch, *Poetry with a Purpose: Biblical Poetics and Interpretation* (Bloomington: Indiana University Press, 1990), 104–35.

7. Hermann Gunkel, *An Introduction to the Psalms* (Macon, GA: Mercer University Press, 1933).

8. See Walter Brueggemann, "The Formfulness of Grief," in *The Psalms and the Life of Faith*, ed. Patrick D. Miller (Minneapolis: Fortress, 1995), 84–97.

9. Claus Westermann, *The Psalms: Structure, Content and Message* (Minneapolis: Augsburg, 1980), 73–83; Claus Westermann, *The Living Psalms* (Grand Rapids: Eerdmans, 1984), 166–200.

10. See Fredrik Lindstrom, *Suffering and Sin: Interpretations of Illness in the Individual Complaint Psalms*, ConBOT 37 (Stockholm: Almqvist & Wiksell, 1994).

11. Walter Brueggemann, *The Message of the Psalms: A Theological Commentary* (Minneapolis: Augsburg, 1984). See also Brueggemann, *Psalms and the Life of Faith*, 3–32.

12. Bernd Janowski, *Arguing with God: A Theological Anthropology of the Psalms* (Louisville: Westminster John Knox, 2013).

13. Claus Westermann (*Praise and Lament in the Psalms* [Atlanta: John Knox, 1981], 25–30) has offered a shrewd discussion concerning the relationship between praise and thanks and the important distinction between the two.

14. Jason Byassee, *Praise Seeking Understanding: Reading the Psalms with Augustine* (Grand Rapids: Eerdmans, 2007).

15. Brevard S. Childs, "Psalm Titles and Midrashic Exegesis," *JSS* 16 (1971): 143.

16. Brevard S. Childs, *Introduction to the Old Testament as Scripture* (Philadelphia: Fortress, 1979), 522.

17. Ernesto Cardenal, *Salmos* (Buenos Aires, 1969), quoted by Enrique Dussel, *Ethics of Liberation in the Age of Globalization and Exclusion*, trans. Eduardo Mendieta et al. (Durham: Duke University Press, 2013), 243. Dussel's accompanying note 276 merits close attention.

18. More than would I, Childs (*Introduction to the Old Testament*, 517–18) accents the eschatological intention of the Psalter.

Chapter 5: Preaching from the Wisdom Traditions

1. Charles Taylor, *Sources of the Self: The Making of the Modern Identity* (Cambridge, MA: Harvard University Press, 1992), 218.

2. Taylor, *Sources of the Self*, 221.

3. Taylor, *Sources of the Self*, 221.

4. Taylor, *Sources of the Self*, 227 (quoting *Paradise Lost* 8.2.192–94).

5. Wendell Berry, *The World-Ending Fire: The Essential Wendell Berry*, ed. Paul Kingsnorth (Berkeley, CA: Counterpoint, 2017), 263.

6. Gerhard von Rad, *Wisdom in Israel* (Harrisburg: Trinity, 1993), 65.

7. James Russell Lowell, "Once to Every Man and Nation," *The Boston Courier* (December 11, 1845). It was written as a protest against the US-Mexican War. It recurs in many hymnals and is all over the web.

8. Von Rad, *Wisdom in Israel*, 99–101.

9. Von Rad, *Wisdom in Israel*, 64–65.

10. Davis Hankins, *The Book of Job and the Immanent Genesis of Transcendence* (Evanston, IL: Northwestern University Press, 2014), 86.

11. Carol Newsom, *The Book of Job: A Contest of Moral Imaginations* (Oxford: Oxford University Press, 2009), 168.

12. Samuel E. Balentine, *Job* (Macon, GA: Smyth & Helwys, 2007), 698.

13. Hankins, *Book of Job*, 223.

14. Jack Miles, *God: A Biography* (New York: Vintage, 1996), 11.

SCRIPTURE INDEX

Compelling and timely books on biblical preaching.
Good preaching changes lives!

Working Preacher Books is a partnership between Luther
Seminary, WorkingPreacher.org, and Fortress Press.

Books in the series include:
Preaching from the Old Testament, by Walter Brueggemann